CREATIVE
WOODCARVING
FOR BEGINNERS

BASIC TECHNIQUES + 50 PROJECTS

Reinhold Büdeker, Jörg Hille, Nicola Mazrek,
Mareen Pries & Karsten Selke

LARK
CRAFTS

A Division of Sterling Publishing Co., Inc.
New York / London

Senior Editor: Terry Taylor

Translation: Eric Bye

Art Director: Skip Wade

Cover Designer: Celia Naranjo

Content Design: Heike Wegner

Concept & Project Management for frechverlag, Inc.: Susanne Kuhn

Library of Congress Cataloging-in-Publication Data

Büdeker, Reinhold.
 Creative woodcarving for beginners : basic techniques : 50 projects / Reinhold Büdeker, Jörg Hille, Nicola Mazrek, Mareen Pries and Karsten Selke. -- 1st ed.
   p. cm.
 Includes index.
 ISBN 978-1-60059-586-8 (pb-trade pbk. : alk. paper)
 1. Wood-carving. 2. Wood-carving--Patterns. I. Title.
 TT199.7.B834 2010
 736'.4--dc22

                                        2010003889

10 9 8 7 6 5 4 3 2 1

First Edition

Published by Lark Books, A Division of
Sterling Publishing Co., Inc.
387 Park Avenue South, New York, NY 10016

English translation © 2010, Lark Books, A Division of Sterling Publishing Co., Inc.

Original German edition published as 1x1 Schnitzen
Text and Photography © 2007, frechverlag GmbH, Stuttgart, Germany (www.frech.de) Karsten Selke (page 56 [Burning] and 76 [work step]), Fotostudio Ullrich and Co., Renningen (all other photos of models, materials, and work photos; title page)

This edition is published by arrangement with Claudia Böhme Rights & Literary Agency, Hannover, Germany (www.agency-bohme.com)

Distributed in Canada by Sterling Publishing,
c/o Canadian Manda Group, 165 Dufferin Street
Toronto, Ontario, Canada M6K 3H6

Distributed in the United Kingdom by GMC Distribution Services,
Castle Place, 166 High Street, Lewes, East Sussex, England BN7 1XU

Distributed in Australia by Capricorn Link (Australia) Pty Ltd.,
P.O. Box 704, Windsor, NSW 2756 Australia

If you have questions or comments about this book, please contact:
Lark Books
67 Broadway
Asheville, NC 28801
828-253-0467

Manufactured in China

ISBN 13: 978-1-60059-586-8

For information about custom editions, special sales, premium and corporate purchases, please contact Sterling Special Sales Department at 800-805-5489 or specialsales@sterlingpub.com.

For information about desk and examination copies available to college and university professors, requests must be submitted to academic@larkbooks.com. Our complete policy can be found at www.larkcrafts.com.

CONTENTS

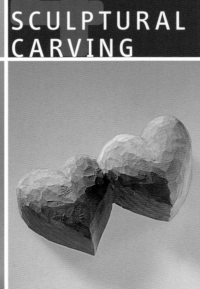

WORKSHOP

Learning Step by Step

This Workshop section is designed to teach the basics of woodcarving step by step, including traditional chip carving, reliefs, lettering, and fully sculptural items such as figures and bowls. After an introduction to the most common carving woods and tools, including chisels and gouges, you will learn each carving technique through thoroughly illustrated instructions.

Project Ideas

The Workshop chapters begin with basic techniques and conclude with a selection of Project Ideas. Each project has easy-to-follow suggestions that will allow you to build your skills repertoire, requiring only those you have acquired up to that point in the book.

Patterns for Help and Direction

You can choose among many paths that can lead to favorite carving methods and projects. Begin with the subjects presented in the book, or simply follow the inspirations of nature, photos, or everyday objects. If you choose to reproduce the models in the book, the necessary patterns and sketches are compiled in easy-to-use formats, starting on page 122.

Note

◆ We recommend going through the Workshop chapter by chapter. The early chapters on chip and relief carving provide a valuable basis for the more demanding figurative and sculptural carving later on. Of course you can also focus on individual techniques where you already have a strong interest.

1 BASICS

Notes

◆ Carving is not without risks, so please follow the instructions and safety recommendations carefully.

◆ Please note that in the chapters A Safe Workspace and Tools & Resources, the utensils listed in the Project Ideas are not mentioned again, so you may want to note their location. In addition, you should have the basic equipment for sharpening chisels and gouges before starting work.

Woodcarving is a challenging and enjoyable skill. Seeing a unique work of art gradually emerge from a simple piece of wood is not only rewarding, but it stimulates the imagination to find in the wood a never-ending world of new shapes and ideas.

To build a firm foundation of skills for your own first carving project, we recommend that you go carefully through the basics in this chapter. You will learn the most important qualities of wood and find guidance in setting up your workplace. You don't need a particularly extensive—or expensive—tool set to get started. The focus is more properly on safety, since dealing with saws, chisels, and mallets is not always free of risk.

Once you have become familiar with the most common chisels and gouges and mastered some simple exercises, you can start to plan your own first creations. Whether you want to carve a specific subject from the book or already have your own idea, the following chapter will show you step by step how to create successful projects.

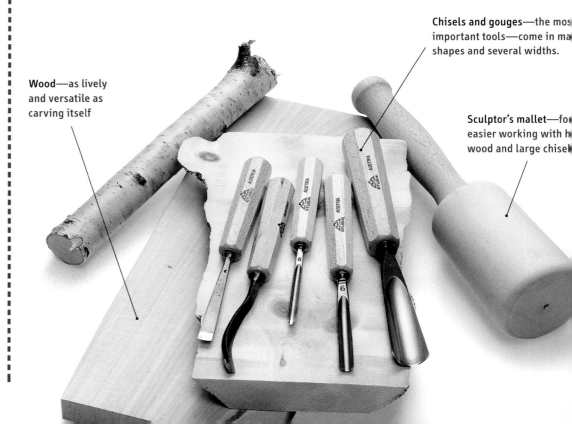

Chisels and gouges—the mos[t] important tools—come in ma[ny] shapes and several widths.

Wood—as lively and versatile as carving itself

Sculptor's mallet—fo[r] easier working with h[ard] wood and large chise[ls]

WOOD AS A LIVING MATERIAL

Wood is the most alive and versatile of all natural materials available to the crafter. No matter how small, every piece is unique in makeup and character. Before presenting some common and popular wood species in the following chapter, we begin with some important details about wood as a living material.

The Structure of Wood

Bark

Annual Rings

Sapwood

Pith

Heartwood

The "heart" of a tree is the cell tissue called *cambium* that is responsible for the formation of new wood. Because the cambium reacts to climate change, it acts as a kind of diary for every tree, reflecting the conditions and circumstances of its growth. The layer of wood that is formed during a growth period is called an *annual ring* (see illustration at left). Since fairly large amounts of sap are transported through the trunk to the crown at the beginning of a growth period, the transporting cells have thinner walls and larger hollow spaces. Later in the year, when the flow of sap decreases, the cells grow thicker, sturdier walls. This change is shown clearly by color variations in the annual rings. Some types of wood also experience a difference in cut resistance, which affects carvability. A cross-section cut through a trunk clearly shows the structure of the wood. The outermost layer is the *outer bark*. Then come the inner bark, also known as the *phloem*, and the very thin cambium. The inner cells of the cambium produce *sapwood* which carries food from roots to leaves, while the outer cells produce bark. As the cells in the cambium continually divide, older sapwood cells get further from the cambium and, through chemical and physical processes, form thickening, inactive *heartwood*. At the center of the trunk is a small core of *pith*.

Fiber Direction and Grain

Fiber direction refers to the orientation of the wood fibers with respect to the long axis of the trunk. It's often relatively straight, but sometimes wavy and irregular. The *grain,* or the texture of the wood, refers to the appearance that is determined by *medullary rays*, annual rings, grain direction, and other structural characteristics (see illustration at right). The grain varies with distance from the bark. Pronounced graining can be a good choice for large or simple carvings, but are not suitable for models with a pattern.

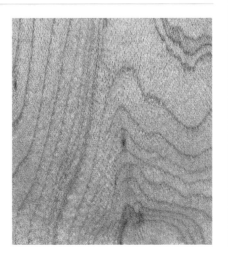

Tips & Tricks

◆ Wood stacked up to dry should be kept in the shade, not the sun, with a cover over the pile. The drying wood should have exposure to good ventilation, but not windy drafts. The goal is for the wood to dry slowly enough that the moisture escapes at a steady rate. This should eliminate tensions inside the wood and prevent cracking.

◆ Wood that is felled in the summer or tends toward splitting can be sealed with beeswax or paraffin.

Drying and Storage

Freshly cut wood contains a good deal of water. As it dries, it loses volume and contracts. It can be worked only after the moisture content falls below about 15 percent. To reach this degree of dryness, it must be stored in fresh air for a long time under the right conditions. Once wood is purchased, it must usually be stored and dried again for two to three weeks indoors at room temperature before it can be worked.

Wood Defects and Damage

Weather-related damage, improper storage, or other causes may produce flaws or other damage that make wood unusable. Other troublesome challenges include twisted grain, which usually occurs in trees exposed to strong winds, and cross grain, when the annual rings run in concentric wave lines with even curves. This type of wood is not appropriate for carving, for it takes a lot of practice to cut the constantly changing direction of the fibers. Other wood types may have unusable sapwood, and you should make sure that it's not too wide or infested with pests. Finally, wood quality can be reduced by splits caused by frost or lightning strikes, as well as insect damage. Branch locations or knots can also detract from the quality of the wood and make it difficult to cut, but wood without branches is scarcely to be found. Sometimes, of course, it's possible to work a branch or other flaw into the design.

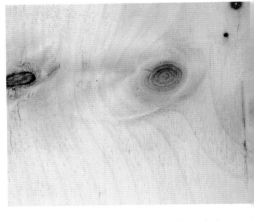

THE RIGHT CARVING WOOD

good number of woods are appropriate for carving. Among the favorite softwoods are bass-
ood, birch, alder, Swiss stone pine, and Eastern white pine. Popular hard carving woods
clude oak, plum, elm, maple, and chestnut. The choice of wood depends mainly on the type of
bject to be carved. The final surface (see chapter 6) should also be considered in choosing a
ood. Many woods are difficult to obtain or very expensive, such as tropical species, and will
ot be considered in this book.

he most common woods that are good for working are presented in the following overview:

Eastern White Pine (*Pinus strobus*)

The wood has a pale yellow to light brown color, sometimes with a slight tinge of red. It shows a fine, even structure and straight grain. Annual rings are not very pronounced. The wood from an Eastern white pine is light, dries fast, and is very good to work with. With increasing age the wood darkens considerably.

wiss Stone Pine (*Pinus cembra*)

e Swiss stone pine is a heartwood tree. The narrow sapwood
yellowish, and the heartwood is reddish and becomes quite
rk. The wood contains lots of resin, and is soft, tough, very
urable, and pleasantly fragrant. At comparable hardness, it's
ronger than the wood of the Eastern white pine.

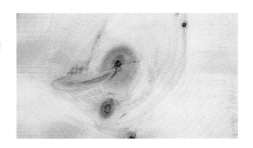

Basswood

This wood is among the most popular and most commonly used woods for carving. It is distinguished by a whitish to brownish coloration without prominent grain. Basswood is soft but tough, and it's especially good for fairly small subjects, details, and lettering.

ak

e wood has a light yellowish-brown color and generally is
raight-grained. Its traits are closely connected to the
owth of the tree: wood that grew quickly is often lighter
d less strong. Wood that grew slowly is dense and hard,
d thus more difficult to work.

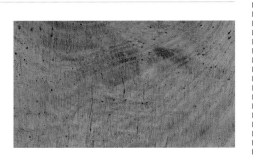

Notes

◆ Many wood sculptors avoid using woods that have become scarce through overcutting.

Tips & Tricks

◆ Ask a carpenter for small scraps cut from beams; you can carve your first items from them and develop a feel for the wood.

Maple

The maple tree produces a light-colored and usually straight-grained wood that dries slowly but well. The wood of the sycamore maple is among the most valuable of the fine hardwoods. It's yellowish-white to white in color; the annual rings are easy to see; and the sapwood and heartwood are not distinguishable, but rather alike in color. This medium-hard, elastic, tough, hardwood shrinks little and has good bending strength. The surface of the wood takes a good finish, is easy to smooth, and takes stain and dye well. Varnish can also be used without difficulty.

Birch

Birch is a finely structured and nearly white wood. Generally it's distinguished by straight grain with nearly no figure. Birch is a very heavy wood that is tough and good to work.

Alder

Freshly cut alder has a pale color, and under the effects of air and light it takes on a glowing orange-brown coloration. The wood has a fine structure but not much grain. Alder dries to be lightweight; it's easy to cut and work as long as the cutting tools are sharp. The wood is not durable.

Fruit Woods

PEAR An ideal carving wood with light reddish-brown coloration and a unified, fine structure. The wood dries slowly and is subject to warping, particularly with irregular grain. It is very tough and difficult to split.

APPLE This is a pale to medium reddish-brown wood with a very fine structure, but not quite as fine as pear. This makes it a particularly good choice for precisely detailed work. The hard, strong wood is tough and difficult to split. It cuts well and takes a good finish.

PLUM The color of the wood varies between reddish-brown and purple-brown, and the sapwood is yellowish. The wood is hard, dense, and brittle. It shrinks significantly and is not durable outdoors. Plum wood works and cuts cleanly.

PROCESSED FORMS OF CARVING WOODS

Trunk Wood

Trunk wood is the least processed form of carving wood. Wood product companies can provide tips on buying. Pay close attention to their information on proper drying and storage, as well as damage and flaws in the wood.

Boards

A board is a piece of wood sawn from a trunk and is at least 1/4 to 1 1/2 inches (6 mm to 3.8 cm) thick.

Planks

A plank is a piece of wood that is sawn from a trunk and is at least 1 1/2 inches (3.8 cm) thick.

Rough-cut Blank

A rough-cut blank is a piece of wood sawn out roughly to its outline. You you may want to ask a carpenter to do this.

A SAFE WORKPLACE

The ideal situation for carving is a separate workplace or room. There you can keep all the essential tools within reach and clearly laid out. Even if there is not separate room for your hobby you can still set up your own workplace.

The most important workplace feature, in addition to a sturdy wooden bench or woodworking bench, is bright, even lighting that can be adjusted depending on the type of carving being done. You will find out which type of lighting you prefer when you do your first practice carvings.

Notes

◆ The heart of a well-equipped, spacious woodworking workshop is a workbench (see photo at left). It must be very stable and sturdy, of a height that suits the user, and with a level top surface. The traditional woodworking bench has two vises or clamping jaws as well as *bench stops* that fit into square recesses in the bench top. These are good especially for clamping fairly long pieces of wood. Often necessary tools and utensils, marking devices, and so forth can be kept in the stand for the bench.

◆ A tile, concrete, or stone floor should be covered with carpet, linoleum, or a rubberized floor covering. That way a dropped chisel will not dull as quickly or suffer damage.

◆ A collapsible workbench is more stable if you keep one foot on the adjustable step. But because of the relatively light construction, the bench is not well suited for working on fairly large, solid pieces while using a sculptor's mallet (see page 16).

Folding Workbench

If you value a workbench but have little room, you should choose a space-saving foldable one, of which there are many available on the market. Some models come equipped with a clamping device (wooden vise jaws or plastic stops; see photo), and they can also be set up with a clamping jig.

The Clamping Device

A movable clamping device is useful for screwing down smaller work pieces. The clamping device can be attached to various surfaces up to 3 inches (7.6 cm) thick. This makes it possible to work even at the kitchen table. The support surface to which the wood being worked is tightly screwed can be turned and secured in any number of positions.

Tips & Tricks

◆ Working with saws and carving tools is not without risks. Always keep a first aid kit available in your workplace.

Notes

◆ On saws, a small number of large teeth widely separated from one another cut quickly, but they also tear the wood. Small, fine teeth produce a finer cut.

◆ In making precise cuts, note that the saw blade—especially a fine-toothed one—will always try to follow the direction of the wood fibers.

TOOLS & RESOURCES

Basic Equipment

Pencils, an eraser, tracing paper, and cardboard are useful for transferring patterns, preparing templates, or making your own blueprints. With a ruler you can measure pieces of wood, planks, and boards and mark out rectangular shapes. A steel rule is a bit more precise. It's finely graduated and can also be used for making straight lines. A *try square* is used to draw and check right angles. To scribe a line you place the shorter part of the tool on the edge of the work piece and run a pencil along the longer extension. Dividers are essential for drawing circles and round or contoured shapes, such as when cutting along a curve.

Scroll Saw and Folding Saw

A scroll saw is fine for cutting wood up to about 1 inch (2.5 cm) thick. One important measurement with a scroll saw is the *throat*; this is the distance between the saw blade and the back of the saw. This limits the depth of the cut when the work is turned. A lock-back folding saw can be used for sawing smaller pieces of wood and branches.

Electric Drill, Hammer, Clamps, and Other Tools

An electric or a cordless drill is used to bore holes quickly and easily for securing work pieces to a jig. Twist drills made from high-performance steel are the right choice for drill bits. Special brad-point woodworking bits have a centering point and cutters on the face. These keep the drill from wandering in the hole. Woodworking bits are available in a variety of sizes, down to 1/8 inch (3 mm).

Broken or split pieces of wood can be attached with wood glue. Common wood glue requires several hours to harden. Quick-drying glue works faster, and sets after a few minutes. If a glued carving project is to be kept outdoors, waterproof wood glue should be used.

Pieces joined with wood glue are clamped in place until the glue is dry. Adhesive tape works well for clamping very small pieces; slip-jaw clamps and spring clamps are used for larger pieces. A hammer is used to position work pieces more precisely in clamps.

Tips & Tricks

◆ An economical alternative to an electric or a cordless drill is a hand drill.

◆ For smoothing fairly large surfaces, sandpaper may be backed with a cork sanding block or a piece of wood.

◆ Don't cut sandpaper with a knife or scissors, which will become dull. It's better to lay the paper on the edge of the bench and tear off a piece with a downward motion.

◆ It's best to use sandpaper after the carving work is done. Pieces of grit from the sandpaper that get lodged in the wood can quickly dull the chisels.

Caution!

Use sandpaper sparingly, because the resulting dust—a mix of wood fibers and abraded grit—can be a health hazard. The dust must be vacuumed up or knocked away.

Sandpaper, Files, and Rasps

Sandpaper, also referred to as emery paper, is used to smooth and clean wood surfaces. Sandpaper comes in various grits, with a number printed on the back: the higher the number, the finer the sandpaper.

A file is used for deburring, rounding edges, and shaping surfaces of the item being carved. If a very rough, coarse structure is desired, a coarse *rasp* is the right choice. A file has teeth in a continuous row. A *single-cut file* is used for soft wood; the row of teeth forms a continuous succession. For harder material, a *double-cut file* is the right choice; its teeth cross one another. With rasps, the cut is made by individual standing teeth, which can take off lots of wood quickly. Both files and rasps are used on the push, moving away from the body. The work piece must thus be clamped firmly.

Files and rasps are available in many different shapes and sizes. Their names are derived from their cross sections, so there are such things as flat, tapered flat, half-round, three-cornered, and round files.

THE MOST IMPORTANT CARVING TOOLS

In woodcarving the most important tool is the chisel or gouge. Carving chisels and gouges come in many different shapes, curvatures, and widths that are used for producing different shapes on the surface of the wood, and which are distinguished by a special numbering system. The numbering, also known as the *cut* or the *sweep*, refers to the curvature of the cutting edge and the blade. The width of the cutting edge is given in fractions of an inch (or millimeters). This chapter provides an introduction to the most important types of chisels used in cutting chips, reliefs, bowls, and figures. There is a helpful overview of the common chisels at the end of this book.

Important Note

◆ Carving chisels and gouges commonly are designated with numbers that indicate their sweep or curvature. This is how the shape of the cuts and the blades is identified. You will find charts on pages 17 and 143 that provide an overview of the basic designations for carving chisels and gouges of the Stubai brand. Cuts 1 through 11 have straight blades with various cut shapes from straight to about half round. Up to the number 20 sweep, the chisels are said to be curved, and up to 32, bent. The overview at the end of the book makes it clear that, for example, the shapes of sweeps 11, 20, and 32 are similar, but the chisels are straight, curved, and bent.

These designations are for orientation, and are by no means universal for all chisel manufacturers. Companies have their own identities and designations and use them to distinguish themselves from other suppliers. Even within a manufacturer there can be deviations in shape. For example, when the chisels are hand forged, it's often possible only to approximate the specified measurements of a sweep.

The Structure of a Chisel

Handle: The handle of a chisel is often made of ash or beech. It can be round or faceted.

Blade: This must be forged from high-grade steel. The blade consists of the top, the back, and the bevel.

Cutting edge: The sharp part of the bevel. The width is specified in fractions of an inch or millimeters. The bevel is the portion of the blade back that has been ground to a specific angle.

Top: The polished side of the blade

Bolster: A support that keeps the blade from being forced too far into or through the handle (such as while working with a sculptor's mallet).

Sweep number

Tang: This is set deeply into the handle. The tang runs along the long axis of the blade.

Ferrule: Made of metal. Keeps the tang from splitting out of the wood under pressure.

Chip Carving Knife and Chisels

The traditional chip carving knife consists of a short, sturdy blade with a stiff tip. As the name indicates, this knife is mainly for chip carving—cutting chips into the wood. The knife pictured here is also known as a bench knife. These chisels have a straight, flat cutting edge. They are available with a straight or angled cutting edge and are often used for chip carving. Chisels are designated with cuts 1 (straight) and 2 (skew) and come in different widths.

Chip carving knife

Straight and skew chisels

Shallow Sweep Gouges

Shallow sweep gouges have slightly curved cutting edges and are designated as sweeps 3, 4, and 5. The higher the number, the greater the curvature of the cutting edge. These are available in various widths. Shallow sweep gouges are often used for basic surface removal. Cuts with very shallow cutting edges are used for setting in and working on large figures, such as from a tree trunk.

Medium Sweep Gouges

These carving gouges are sweeps 6 through 8, and they have more pronounced curvature than the shallow gouges. The various cuts are used for smoothing surfaces and for wood removal. Medium sweep gouges are part of the basic equipment of every carver and are used very frequently.

U-gouges

U-gouges have a very pronounced curve. With these tools, which are designated with sweeps 9 through 11, in increasing curvature, the cutting edge is formed in the shape of a semi-circle. Sweep 11, the one with the deepest curve, is in the shape of a U. U-gouges are very good for carving grooved recesses and for background cuts, such as with high relief and figures, because as the blade is turned in the wood, it produces no splinters.

Carving chisels and gouges are traditional products that are subject to continuous changes in designation. Beginning carvers will find few criteria for evaluating the quality of the steel or the manageability of the tools. Even for experienced carvers, part of the buying decision depends on emotional factors in addition to the physically measurable technical features. Seek out competent advice that takes into account your interests and current knowledge, and communicates the choices reasonably and convincingly. Some important questions you must consider are: For what project do I need a minimum number of chisels? At what price? What alternatives are there?

◆ Blades and handles or *grips* can also be bought separately. In any case, ask your dealer to install the selected handles.

Notes

◆ You will produce very good results over time and enjoy the work only if you use high-quality chisels. So make sure you don't buy any substandard tools, for such chisels seldom last long and frequently need sharpening, which is very time-consuming.

◆ A few tools will be adequate at the beginning. Many manufacturers offer special beginners' sets (such as six- or twelve-piece sets) that can be used for chip cutting and relief work, as well as figures and bowls. But experience shows that such kits often contain one chisel or gouge that you will rarely use. On page 17 you will find a recommendation for a basic kit of carving chisels and gouges.

Special Shapes

Parting tools, also known as V-gouges because of the shape of their blade, are tools that work very well for carving lines and corners. The cutting edges of a V-tool can be arranged in angles from acute to obtuse. Angles of 45°, 60°, 75°, and 100° are usual.

Places that are hard to reach can be carved with bent and curved chisels, which are available in cuts 1 through 11 as well as with V-tools. With curved chisels the entire blade is slightly bent. Bent chisels are ones in which the blade is bent only in the forward part. They are especially suited for carving bowls and recesses.

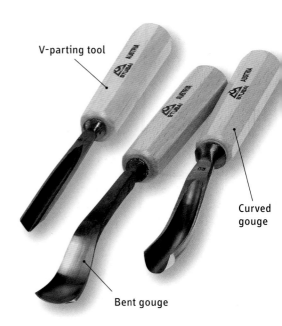

V-parting tool

Curved gouge

Bent gouge

Sculptor's mallet

When you want to remove lots of wood, or work very hard wood, sometimes it's helpful to drive the chisel or gouge into the wood with a sculptor's mallet. This is also recommended for performing small, precise cuts. A sculptor's mallet has a heavy cylindrical head that can be used to strike the end of the tool's handle at any angle (for use of the sculptor's mallet, see also page 21, step 5).

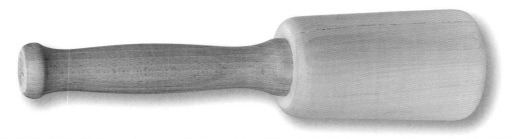

Storing the Tools

Since the cutting edges of the chisels are very delicate, it's essential to use and store the tools carefully. The chisels should never be kept loose in a drawer or a box, for the sharpened edges would come into contact with one another and quickly get damaged or dulled. A box with an insert is ideal, in which the chisels can be placed parallel to one another.

A simple, practical alternative is a tool roll in which the pockets for the chisels are offset so that the cutting edges are protected between the handles of the opposing tools.

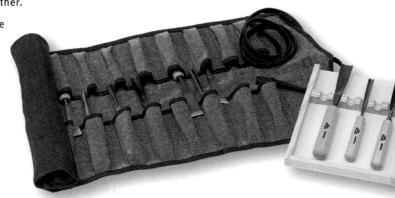

CHISELS & GOUGES—BASIC EQUIPMENT

The chart below provides an overview of the collective terms for various types of chisels and gouges (chisels to U-gouges) plus the cuts they make (sweeps 1 through 32).

Chisels and gouges are always designated with the sweep and the width of the cutting edge. This width is measured from corner to corner, so no. 3 sweep ³⁄₈-inch (10 mm) designates a shallow gouge with a 3 sweep and a cutting edge ³⁄₈ inch (10 mm) wide.

All the models proposed in the Workshops and Project Ideas can be carved with the cuts (Basic Chisels) provided in the right side of the chart. In addition you will need a ³⁄₁₆-inch (5 mm) V-gouge with a 45° angle, as well as a chip carving knife (bench knife). Important: All sweep designations in this chart refer to chisels of the Stubai brand. The different designations for other manufacturers (see Note on pages 14–15) are of no consequence to the projects presented in the book. Since the use of chisels is a totally individual matter and will change continually with increasing practice and experience, the basic equipment presented here should not be considered a "required purchase," but rather a helpful, economical set for beginners with no previous knowledge and carving tools. Variations in sweep designations come into play with professional decorative carving, the precise elaboration of filigree shapes (such as leaf motifs and volutes), or when the carving work must not deviate from the historical pattern (such as in restoration work).

	Designations of Stubai Chisels Available Cut Shapes			Basic Chisels and Gouges All projects in Workshops and Project Ideas can be done with these chisels and gouges.		
	Straight Sweep	Curved Sweep	Bent Sweep	Straight	Curved	Bent
Chisels	1 Sweep	–	21 Sweep			21 Sweep ⁵⁄₁₆-inch (8 mm)
	2 Sweep	–	22 Sweep 23 Sweep	2 Sweep ³⁄₈-inch (10 mm)		
Shallow Gouges	3 Sweep	–	–	3 Sweep ³⁄₁₆-inch (5 mm) 3 Sweep ³⁄₈-inch (10 mm) 3 Sweep ⁵⁄₈-inch (16 mm)		
	4 Sweep	12 Sweep	24 Sweep	4 Sweep 1-inch (25 mm)		
	5 Sweep	14 Sweep	26 Sweep	5 Sweep ⁵⁄₁₆-inch (8 mm) 5 Sweep ¹⁄₂-inch (13 mm) 5 Sweep ³⁄₄-inch (19 mm)		
Medium Sweep Gouges	6 Sweep	–	–			
	7 Sweep	16 Sweep	28 Sweep	7 Sweep ³⁄₈-inch (10 mm)	16 Sweep ⁵⁄₈-inch (16 mm)	
	8 Sweep	–	–			
U-Gouges	9 Sweep	18 Sweep	30 Sweep	9 Sweep ⁵⁄₁₆-inch (8 mm)	18 Sweep ¹⁄₂-inch (13 mm)	
	10 Sweep	–	–	10 Sweep ¹⁄₄-inch (6 mm) 10 Sweep ³⁄₈-inch (10 mm)		
	11 Sweep	20 Sweep	32 Sweep	11 Sweep ¹⁄₁₆-inch (2 mm) 11 Sweep ³⁄₄-inch (19 mm)	20 Sweep ⁷⁄₁₆-inch (11 mm)	

addition: ³⁄₁₆-inch and ³⁄₈-inch 45° V-gouges (45° / 5 and 10 mm) plus a chip carving knife

Tips & Tricks

◆ When you buy chisels and gouges, pay attention to the quality of the ferrule. With a ferrule on the outside there is more wood between the ferrule and the tang than with an inner ferrule. Since wood is flexible, sometimes the tang can break through a handle with an outer ferrule when subjected to long-term stress. If you use your chisels and gouges very frequently, types with inner ferrules are the best choice.

◆ Large chisels and gouges that are struck with a mallet last longer when the striking end is well protected. A striking knob that you install is helpful in distributing the pressure over the entire end. Simply glue a furniture glide from a hardware store in the center of a handle end with a pre-drilled pilot hole.

Notes

◆ The angle ground on the chisel or gouge is called the *bevel*. As an approximation, the bevel (sharpening angle) for soft wood can be specified as falling between 15° and 25°; for hardwood, an angle of 25° to 35° is recommended. Generally, the bevel should be as small as possible.

◆ Sharpening stones are usually sold as rectangular blocks that can be attached to the workbench or a jig.

◆ Long cut stones are available in several different profiles. Depending on the shape of the sweep being sharpened, you can use square, triangular, half-round, round, or teardrop-shaped sharpening stones.

Tips & Tricks

◆ You can also buy combination stones, in which two stones of different grits are cemented together. There are also combinations of natural and synthetic abrasive stones.

Sharpening Chisels & Gouges

Sharp chisels make it possible to work accurately, tirelessly, and safely. A uniformly ground bevel is a requirement. Since the delicate cutting edges wear down quickly or can become damaged, regular sharpening is essential to carve successfully. The sharpening process is divided into two steps: grinding and honing. Chisels can be sharpened both by hand and with an electric (wet) grinder, which is simpler and faster.

Hand Sharpening

For sharpening chisels and gouges with straight or curved cutting edges, sharpening stones that are impregnated with water or oil are a particularly good choice. The steel glides on them, and small, abraded particles are rinsed off.

Step-by-Step Instructions

Grinding the Bevel with a Combination Waterstone

Soak the waterstone thoroughly and attach it so that the rough side is up. The gouge—like the shallow sweep gouge in the photo—is moved gently over the waterstone in circular motions. Use the other hand to apply gentle pressure on the forward part of the blade. Depending on the sweep, the chisel should be rocked left and right while sharpening. The result is a noticeably rough surface on the bevel.

1

Fine Grinding on the Bevel

Perform the grinding process on the fine side (400-grit) of the stone. Wet the top of the stone with water and run the bevel over it in circular and sidewise motions. This produces a fine abrasion of the steel that gives a sharp cutting edge. The better the first grind is done, the quicker and simpler will be the fine grinding.

2

Deburring the Top Side

The grinding produces a fine burr along the entire cutting edge, which must be removed. A shaped stone with a profile that fits the shape of the chisel or gouge being sharpened is placed on the top side and run over the stone in circular motions. Check with your finger or do a trial cut to see if any of the burr is still present.

3

Removing the Burr on the Bevel Side (Honing)

4 The burr remaining on the bevel is removed using an abrasive stone (such as an oil or water Arkansas stone) or a leather *strop*. To polish the chisel, pull it toward you by the handle, keeping the tool at a consistent angle.

Sharpening with a Bench Grinder

Chisels and gouges can be sharpened much more quickly and precisely with a wet grinding machine. Even complicated shapes such as bent chisels can be ground and honed. Since the grindstone runs in water, the cutting edge is cooled as it's ground, so there is no overheating of the steel. Since no sparks are produced, it's possible to work even in areas where there is a fire danger.

Step-by-Step Instructions

Grinding with a Water-Cooled Stone

1 Place the chisel or gouge to be sharpened in the grinding jig on the machine, turn the machine on, and place the bevel side of the chisel on the stone.

Rocking Motion While Grinding

2 During the grinding operation, continually and slowly rock the bevel from side to side.

Occasionally check the results of the grinding by removing the chisel from the grinding jig. This jig makes it possible to return the tool to the same position and the same angle for further grinding.

Honing on a Leather Strop

3 To remove the burr, apply a polishing paste to the leather. Secure the carving chisel in the holding jig and place it on the leather. Since the approach angle of the holding device remains constant, the burr is honed off in just a couple of seconds at the same angle that it was ground. The result is a razor-sharp cutting edge.

Note

◆ Make sure that the grindstone does not stand in water for a long time when the machine is not on. Since the stone soaks up water, over time this will produce an imbalance that will result in an irregular grind in subsequent use.

Tips & Tricks

◆ A practical alternative to sharpening with a water-cooled grinder is to use a machine with a slow-turning grindstone that is not cooled by water (manmade stone). The resulting burr on the cutting edge, which is larger than with a water-cooled grinder, can be removed by, for example, an Arkansas stone. The chisel is held with one hand while the other hand holds the stone and moves it back and forth over the chisel. In this procedure, the stone must not tip over the cutting edge and round it off, or it will have to be applied alternately on the bevel and the topside.

◆ With machines that turn at high speed there is a danger that the heated cutting edge will be annealed and become brittle.

Note

◆ Practice makes perfect! The more you experiment with chisels, gouges, and different types of wood, the quicker and better you will learn their strong points and find the best way to work with them. When you are secure in the basic techniques, progress toward more advanced skills comes quickly.

Tips & Tricks

◆ A pair of crossed band-aids can reduce blistering on the palm of the hand.

Using Chisels & Gouges

Before you start carving the models described in the Workshop, you should become familiar with how to handle a chisel. This section will walk you through the prerequisites for proper use and mastery of your basic tools.

Step-by-Step Instructions

Mounting the Piece of Wood onto a Jig

Screw the holding plate to the carving wood using a screwdriver or a cordless drill with a screwdriver bit.

1a

Screwing the Holding Plate to the Jig

Turn the plate over and place it onto the retainer on the jig. Screw the holding plate securely to the jig from underneath.

1b

Placing the Handle in the Hand

Grip the chisel or gouge so the palm can exert pressure on the tool and the tool lies securely in the hand.

Determine what kind of grip you feel most comfortable with.

2

Controlling a Cut

One hand grips the handle as shown above and the other hand holds the blade. The ball of the hand on the blade should contact the work piece so that one hand pushes and the other "brakes" to keep the chisel under control at all times. If it's not possible to rest the ball of the hand, the forearm should rest firmly against the bench top or the work piece.

3

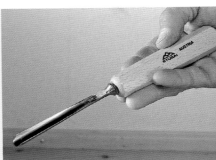

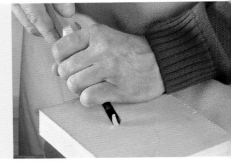

Limiting the Cut

4 This technique is especially helpful for fine, detailed carving. Here the right hand (or the left, for left-handed people) holds the handle, and the index finger of the left (or right) hand is placed against the work piece to form a stop. This way you can use the forward part of the blade to precisely direct and guide the movement of the chisel or gouge, and the tool and the hand cannot slip on the wood.

Working with the Sculptor's Mallet

5 Place the blade of the chisel or gouge at the desired angle on the wood and drive the mallet in short, firm blows onto the end of the handle. Keep control of the angle and the direction of the blade by slightly turning and arching your wrist during the striking motion.

Tips & Tricks

◆ You don't have to stick to the holds and guidelines presented here. After a short while and a little practice you will find that a particular hold is more or less comfortable, and you may be able to work more effectively with an "unconventional" approach.

Notes

◆ Note the difference between *grain* and *fiber*. Grain designates the overall appearance of a wood surface and refers to the visible diversity of adjacent fibers. The fibers are the elongated, pointed structures that comprise the majority of cells in the tree.

◆ This "feel" of wood fiber is clearly demonstrated by holding a thick, round paintbrush. If you stroke the bristles from the ferrule to the ends, they feel smooth. If you stroke in the opposite direction, from the ends of the hairs to the ferrule, there is a perceptible resistance, and the hairs of the brush will stick out or crumple.

HOW WOOD GRAIN AFFECTS THE CUT

When wood is split, grooves, lines, and long fibrous splinters become visible. Just like the hairs of a paintbrush, the bundles of fibers run parallel in the trunk. They provide the tree with strength. A log can easily be split along the grain, but it's difficult to split across it. So in boards and planks the fibers always run parallel to the long edge. This produces an important basic rule for carving:

Cutting with the Grain

The black arrows in the photo indicate the direction of the wood grain. It's easy to cut the wood along or parallel to the grain. Cutting "with the grain" means always cutting from the highest point of the work to a lower one.

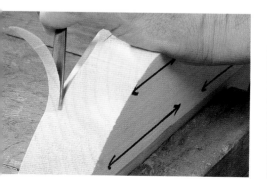

Cutting across and against the Grain

If cutting is done across or even against the grain—in this example, from low to high—the wood splits. A smooth, clean cut is not possible.

Tips & Tricks

◆ If you don't have a photocopier, you can enlarge the patterns using a grid. On a sheet of paper the same size as the origi-nal subject (see the specified height or size), draw a grid of the specified dimen-sions, preferably with graph paper. After drawing the grid, the pattern can be trans-ferred square by square. It's best to work with a pencil (HB) so you can make quick corrections if a line is not right at first.

Transferring Patterns and Designing Your Own Subjects

In the following chapter you will learn various ways to visualize given subjects and your own ideas, from drawing a subject to your own free conception.

Determining the Size of the Piece of Wood

For the models proposed in this book you will find precise measurements for the necessary pieces of wood in the materials list. If you want to work on sub-jects you come up with on your own, you must first determine the precise length and width of your item. Figure in at least enough wood so that you can clamp the piece securely to work on it. But the piece of wood should not be significantly larger than the final ver-sion, otherwise you will have to remove or saw off an excessive amount of wood.

Enlarging Patterns

Normally the patterns are shown in reduced size in the book. But you can easily enlarge them with the speci-fied copy factor. That way you produce the actual size of the pattern. This is specified in the materials list for the piece under *Subject Size*.

Alternatively, you can have copies made on a photo-copier. With particularly large subjects, trace the pat-tern, divide it into several pieces, and put them back together after enlarging.

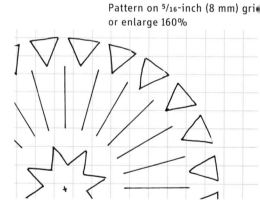

Pattern on $5/16$-inch (8 mm) gri or enlarge 160%

Transferring with Carbon and Tracing Paper

Place the tracing paper over the copied, enlarged pat-tern and trace it. Place the carbon paper with the coated side contacting the wood and the tracing paper on top of it. Secure everything with cellophane tape and trace over the lines with a pencil. This transfers the pattern clearly onto the wood. This transfer method is particularly appropriate when many small details are to be carved.

Transferring with Templates

Using a pencil, transfer the pattern to tracing paper, and then glue the tracing paper onto thin cardboard and cut it out. Place the resulting template onto the wood and use a soft pencil to scribe around the outline. This transfer method is appropriate especially for small subjects with simple, clear outlines, and when an item is to be carved in multiple copies.

Using Photos as Patterns

Perhaps you have a specific topic you like and don't know how to translate it into a carving. First determine the desired size of your work piece. Then take a photo from the front and the side in the desired size. Of course you can enlarge or reduce a photo at will on a photocopy machine. Now trace around the outline of the subject as accurately as possible on tracing paper and transfer this to the wood with carbon paper or a template.

WORKING WITH THREE-DIMENSIONAL SHAPES

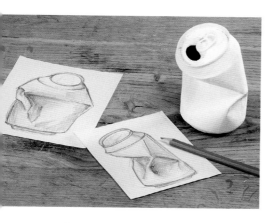

Drawing Freehand

In addition to photography, drawing is a possible way to approximate the individual shape and spatial dimensions of common objects. As shown on page 69, if a crumpled soft drink can is to be carved, it must first be drawn under a concentrated light source to appear three-dimensional. This works best if the can is first painted a single matte color, such as white, so that it's easier to understand the shapes. A drawing of the item from at least two perspectives helps in transferring the shapes more effectively into three dimensions in wood.

Proportions Gauge

Proportions gauges are useful in carving human figures or sculptures. According to a classical model based on the size of the head, the human form is divided into eight units, whereby the nipples, navel, crotch, center of the thigh, fingertips, lower edge of the knee, and center of the calf are all one "head height" from one another. The shoulder width of a man is said to equal two head heights (see sketch in the pattern section on page 122). A rigid classification pattern is not as useful for specific postures and movements, however, because proportions are changed by perspective foreshortening and depth effects.

Notes

◆ In transferring patterns, pay attention to the direction of the wood grain. Fragile parts, such as legs of animals, should run lengthways with the grain, the most stable direction.

◆ Read more about determining the proportions of figures in the chapter Sculptural Carving; see the list of tips starting on page 43.

Tips & Tricks

◆ Instead of blue carbon paper you can also use commonly available black carbon paper. It smudges less on the surface than the blue paper. Pattern paper for sewing projects can be very useful with colored, smooth, or low-contrast wood surfaces. This is available in many colors in hobby shops.

◆ Are you sure you have transferred all the lines of the pattern using blue or black carbon paper? To check, carefully loosen one side of the pattern and lift it up. That way you can check all the sides. But don't remove the pattern entirely, for you won't get it back into place and the missing lines won't be traced precisely.

2 CHIP CARVING

Note

◆ The Vikings practiced what we now call chip carving, skillfully decorating not only common items of daily life but also their weapons and ships with sumptuous runes and other designs.

Chip carving is considered the oldest technique for carving and decorating wood. As the name suggests, chips are cut into the wood to form a graphic pattern, a decoration, or lettering. Through the millennia, chip carving has evolved steadily and today features a wide variety of shapes and patterns that enhance almost anything made of wood, including plates, bowls, boxes, cutting boards, cupboards, doors, and columns.

Chip carving is not only the simplest way to learn carving in a technical sense, but also the most direct route to understanding the many varieties of the craft and gaining a feel for the qualities of wood. With these initial simple exercises you can quickly move toward a sense of the makeup of wood and how it "reacts" to various cuts.

If you have no experience working with wood, we recommend chip carving—and the exercises in this chapter—as the place to begin.

Simply carved basic shapes turn into decorative ornaments.

Chip carving techniques are frequently used for lettering.

Making Decorations

In the following example you will learn three basic types of carving with which you can make numerous decorative shapes. These include the triangular cut, the radius stop cut, and chiseling out circular surfaces. The resulting basic forms can be applied to many decorations.

Step-by-Step Instructions

Transferring the Pattern

1

Transfer the circular pattern on page 122 to the top of the box as described on page 22, using tracing and carbon paper.

Clamping Down the Lid of the Box

2

Secure the top of the box to the holding plate of the jig. Screw three small, appropriately shaped pieces of plywood next to the cover to hold it down firmly while you work on it.

Making a Triangle: First Cut

3a

First cut the triangles on the outside. Using a 45° / 3/16-inch (5 mm) V-gouge, cut a chip from one corner of the triangle inward toward the center. In so doing, always first cut across the grain, and subsequently cut with the grain; otherwise the wood may tear.

Making a Triangle: Second and Third Cuts

3b

Cut in toward the center from the two other corners. If you are not sure how the wood will react, cut in with the V-gouge at an angle of approximately 20° and work up to an angle of 40°. Important: keep the same angle of cut throughout the cutting process.

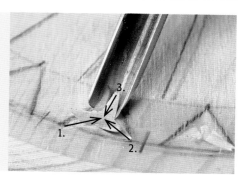

Tips & Tricks

◆ As you create the triangles with the V-gouge, you can make things easier by using a pencil to draw angle bisectors.

Note

◆ In drawing patterns and decorations by hand, you should use a freshly sharpened soft pencil and a clean ruler (ideally a metal rule) that lies totally flat on the wood. Measure precisely and always draw line by line; this makes any needed corrections easier. A good compass with a soft, sharp lead is recommended for rosettes and curved shapes. Make sure that the hole you make with the point of the compass is not too big, for later on it will be difficult to hide.

Making Decorations
Continued

Making Decorations
Continued

Tips & Tricks

◆ To keep all the triangles the same size, you should avoid cutting away the outlines transferred with the carbon paper.

◆ The center of the triangle must be the lowest point, and the edges must always be the highest. The center should not be cut too deep.

Removing Material from the Edge, First Cut

Use a 2 sweep ³/₁₆-inch (5 mm) skew bevel chisel to flatten the face. Place the point of the steel cutting edge in such a way that an even, triangular surface is removed and the point is guided into the center of the triangle. Notice: Cut with the grain to produce a smooth, clean cut.

4a

Removing Material from the Edge, Second and Third Cuts

Work the other two sides of the face of the triangle in the same way. Complete the chip-carved surfaces of all triangles to form an even circle of triangles on the rim of the lid. Try to make the cuts as precise and identical as possible to produce an attractive, even appearance.

4b

Making the Triangles on the Star

Once again chip-carve the triangles in the center of the lid using the V-gouge (see steps 3a and 3b). Then complete the faces with a 2 sweep ³/₁₆-inch (5 mm) (see steps 4a and 4b). As the triangles must touch one another without overlapping, the cuts must be done with particular care.

5

Opening up the Center of the Star

For the center of the star, use a 10 sweep ¹/₄-inch (6 mm) gouge held at a right angle to the box cover; tip it approximately 15° to the side and rotate it around the center several times. The slight tipping as the gouge is turned cuts out a semicircle.

6

Radius Stop Cut—A Border Line Made by Cutting in Vertically

Use the same gouge vertically on the circular line to make half-round cuts. These delimit the previously drawn straight lines.

7a

Carving the Shape out to the Border

Place the same gouge on the other end of the straight lines, cut into the wood, and cut up to the end at the same depth. Note: With every line the cutting angle changes with the direction of the wood grain, so carefully make an initial cut $^1/_{32}$ inch (1 mm) deep and then work it down to a depth of $^3/_{32}$ to $^1/_8$ inch (2 to 3 mm). If necessary, go over the semicircular edging lines again.

Chip Carving Decorations with a Chisel

Instead of using a V-gouge, you can make the initial cuts with a 2 sweep $^3/_{16}$-inch (5 mm) chisel. In this case, draw the angle bisectors for the triangles. As you cut in, the axis of the chisel must be vertical to the top surface of the lid. Now cut the surfaces by cutting with the tip from the sides to the center of the triangle as you hold the chisel at an angle.

Working Continuously

Since the direction of the grain continually changes while you carve out the pattern, a movable clamping device (see page 11) is a good idea, for it allows turning the work piece right in place. This makes it possible for you to work continuously without tedious re-clamping.

Tips & Tricks

◆ When the grain allows, and if the wood is likely to split, you should do the radius stop cut also from the inside and toward the outside.

Chip Carving Letters

◆ For getting started in carving lettering, the best choice is letters that have pointed serifs and straight lines (shafts); pointed serifs are easier to cut in with the chisel than are broad beginnings of letters. With straight lines you can avoid having to frequently change cut direction because of the changes in the grain. Curved lines require turning the chisel and the hand under firm, equal pressure. This technique needs to be practiced before you carve complex lettering.

◆ The steeper the angle of the chisel (40° to 60°), the more expressive the overall image of the script. But the deeper you carve, the harder it is to carve cleanly.

◆ Useful patterns include the common computer scripts. Cursive scripts that communicate lightness and verve are also appropriate for getting started in carving scripts.

Using relatively simple basic techniques of chip carving is also an effective way to make letter and script. But before starting, a few considerations on the layout of letters and the formation of scripts will be helpful. The parts of the letters indicated in the sketch below for the lettering BAD are important for attractive, precise lettering.

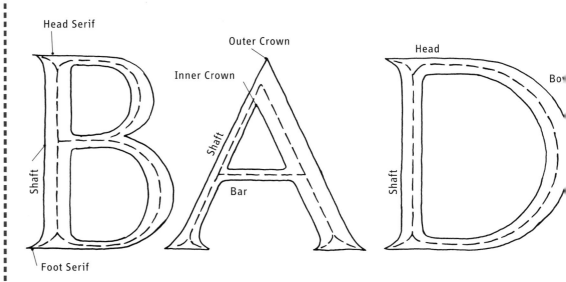

The dotted lines indicate the bottom of the cuts made with the V-gouge.

Step-by-Step Instructions

Transferring the Pattern

1 Transfer the pattern for the script onto the wood and clamp the board securely. A (dotted) center-line in the letters (see sketch above) indicates the deepest part of the cut (see steps 2 through 4).

Preliminary Cuts with the V-gouge

2 Start by cutting in the serifs—the run-outs at the ends of the letters—with the 45° ³/₁₆-inch (45° / 5 mm) V-gouge. Place the V-gouge at a 20° angle on the tip of the serif. Go over the cut to create a cut angle of approximately 40°.

Cutting Straight Lines with the V-gouge

3 Cut in all straight lines along their centerlines with the V-gouge. Make the preliminary cut approximately 1/32 inch (1 mm) deep and then lower them to 1/8 inch (3 mm).

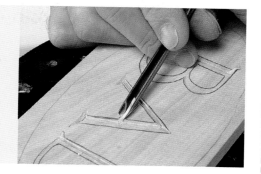

Carving Outside Curves with the V-gouge

4 Use the V-gouge to make a preliminary cut to the same depth on the centerline of the outside curve or the "belly" of the B and the D. Since we should always cut away from our bodies, the chisel must be removed and the board turned on the clamping jig.

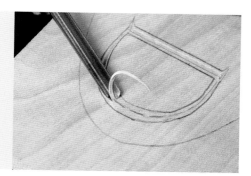

Cutting in the Outside Curve

5a The inward-facing sides of the curves are carved out to the deepened centerline. To keep this neat and exact, use chisels of the right shape. With the B in this type of script and this size, using 7 sweep 3/16-inch (5 mm) and 16 sweep 5/8-inch (16 mm) gouges is recommended; for the broader curve of the D use a 5 sweep 5/16-inch (8 mm).

Cutting out the Inner Curve

5b Make the outside curves with the 3 sweep 3/16-inch (5 mm) chisel. Place the flat side (bevel aligned on the centerline) on the drawn line and cut in at an angle to the cut-in centerline. Carve in the belly of the letter D in the same way.

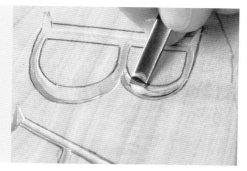

Cutting Out the Shaft from the Side

6 Cut in all straight lines to the pre-cut centerline, specifically the shafts of B, A, and D, plus the crossbar of the A from the outside and the inside, using the same shallow gouge held at an angle. Then cut all crowns and corners so they are neat and free of chips.

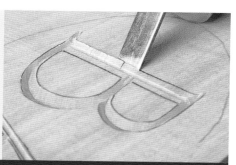

Tips & Tricks

◆ Always make sure to keep the distance between individual letters even and equal. If they are too close together, the effect is unsettling—likewise if they are too far apart or the spacing is uneven. However, there is no ideal measurement for creating a letter, for every letter is located in a specific reference to another. First draw the word or text you intend to carve using guidelines on paper to ascertain the ideal distance between letters. The texture (grain pattern) of the wood used also plays a major role in this. With highly figured wood a greater distance between the letters is helpful in increasing legibility.

BOX

Decorate the lid of the box with the design as described on pages 25–27. Remove any visible lines from the carbon paper with very fine sandpaper.

Tips & Tricks

◆ Design your own decorations on these basic forms and use them to decorate such things as the rim of the box, clothes hangers, cutting boards, and much more.

SIZE
5½ inches (14 cm) in diameter, 4 inches (10.2 cm) tall

MATERIALS
◆ Box made from fir or pine, 5½ inches (14 cm) in diameter

CARVING TOOLS
◆ Chisel: 2 sweep ⅜ inch (10 mm)

◆ U-gouge: 10 sweep ¼-inch (6 mm)

◆ V-gouge: 45° ³⁄₁₆-inch (5 mm)

PATTERN
Page 122

PROJECT IDEAS

SIZE
Approximately 9 x 4¾ inches (22.9 x 12 cm)

MATERIALS
◆ Small piece of beech board approximately 9 x 4¾ inches (22.9 x 12 cm)

CARVING TOOLS
◆ U-gouge: 10 sweep ¼-inch (6 mm)

◆ V-gouge: 45° / ³⁄₁₆-inch (5 mm)

PATTERN
Page 122

NAME PLATE

Clamp the board firmly so it can be worked on. Transfer the decoration and the lettering to the board according to the pattern. Cut in the name with the V-gouge, and use the gouge for the radius stop cut (also see pages 26 and 27, steps 7a and 7 and pages 28 and 29).

Tips & Tricks

◆ Make individual boards for your family members, friends, and acquaintances. There's virtually no limit to the variety of designs you can make with basic shapes and simple carved lines.

SUN WHEEL BOOKENDS

Transfer the pattern to the basswood block and clamp it securely. Cut in a preliminary centerline with the V-gouge (see the description of the triangle on the box lid, pages 25 and 26). Shape the twelve rays with a chisel and carve the notched ends with the V-gouge. Use a chip carving knife to remove any remaining small slivers. Round the center of the sun with a chisel and go over any small slivers with the bench knife.

SIZE
Approximately
3¹⁄₂ inches (9 cm)

MATERIALS FOR EACH BOOKEND
- Basswood block Approximately 2¹⁄₂ x 3¹⁄₂ x 2 inches (6.4 x 8.9 x 5.1 cm)

CARVING TOOLS
- Chip carving knife
- Chisel: 3 sweep ³⁄₁₆-inch (5 mm)
- V-gouge: 45° / ³⁄₁₆-inch (5 mm)

PATTERN
Page 123

CHIP CARVING

SIZE
Approximately 12 inches (30.5 cm) long

MATERIALS
- Spatula made from beech wood, approximately 12 inches (30.5 cm) long

CARVING TOOLS
- Chisel: 3 sweep ³⁄₁₆-inch (5 mm)
- V-gouge: 45° / ³⁄₁₆-inch (5 mm)

PATTERN
Page 122

SPATULA

Secure the ends of the spatula to the workbench with small screw clamps, using a piece of wood or cardboard as a pad to avoid creating small dents with the clamps. Transfer the chip carving pattern and draw in the centerlines for the triangles. Cut these in with a V-gouge. Carve the surfaces sloping to the center of the triangles with a chisel. Use the V-gouge to cut a border around the triangles.

Tips & Tricks

- Since beech is a hardwood, only small chips can be cut out. Keep the cuts shallow.

3 RELIEF CARVING

Notes

♦ A *relief carving* is a sculpture in which the figure is not free-standing but is raised only slightly above a surface. Relief work has been described as "carving pictures in wood."

♦ Relief carving has been well known since antiquity. It was raised to an art form in the 17th and 18th centuries, and continues in popularity today because of its many uses in furniture decoration, sign making, and pictorial wall decoration.

♦ Absolute precision is required in professional relief carving, such as commission work on decorations for house facades and churches. As a result there are few liberties in the choice of carving tools.

In relief carving, no patterns are worked into the wood, as is the case with chip carving; rather, the background surrounding the desired object is cut lower so that the subject moves into the central point. This is how a "raised," pictorial impression is created. Tension, movement, and liveliness are created by varying surface inclinations, tapering lines, and interlacing shapes. With reference to spatial depth, there are two general types of relief carving: in low (or bas) relief, the object stands out from the background only slightly, whereas with high relief the subject is carved from the background to be significantly higher and more sculptural. As with chip carving, using a graphic outline or a pattern can be a helpful foundation in creating a relief from a background. It mirrors the subject in detail and serves as a pattern during the work. The subject need not be copied precisely, but if the carved model doesn't turn out right, compare it to the pattern to see what you can do to correct it.

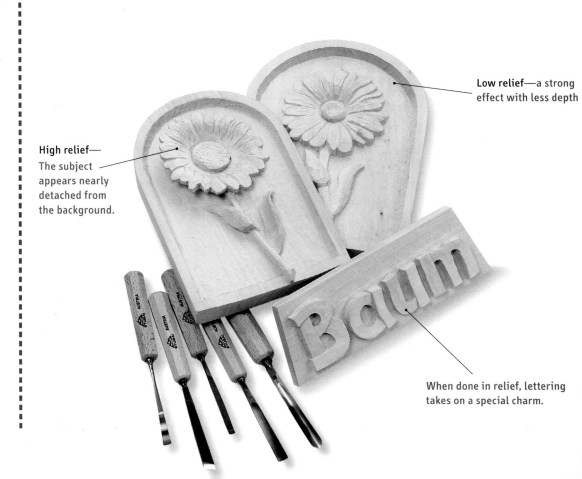

Low relief—a strong effect with less depth

High relief—The subject appears nearly detached from the background.

When done in relief, lettering takes on a special charm.

CARVING LETTERS

Lettering, which we explored in the section on chip carving, is also very decorative when done in relief, as with directional signs. With the chip carving technique, cut letters and scripts with serifs are a good choice, but in designing raised scripts it is better to begin with broad, blocky types. The letters take on verve and lightness through the three-dimensional difference in surface height.

Step-by-Step Instructions

Cutting Around the Script

Transfer the lettering, based on the pattern on page 124, to a 1-inch (2 cm) board and clamp the board down securely. Use a 10 sweep ¼-inch (6 mm) gouge to make a coarse cut around the letters to a depth of approximately ⅜ inch (1 cm). For clearer orientation, it's a good idea to draw a guideline around the edge of the board, parallel to the top and ⅜ inch (1 cm) down (see photo) to act as a depth gauge.

Refining the Outer Contours

Use the 45° / 3/16-inch (5 mm) V-gouge to cut angled chips nearly vertically from the letters. The cuts should be directed to the outside at an angle of approximately 15°. The letters thus get slightly broader near the background.

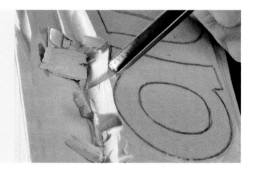

Cutting in the Inner Surfaces

Carve the inner surfaces of the letters. First use the 10 sweep ¼-inch (6 mm) gouge down to the depth, and then cut the angular inside areas with the V-gouge. Do the curves as required with the gouge, the 7 sweep ⅜-inch (10 mm) gouge, or the 16 sweep ⅝-inch (16 mm) curved gouge. Enclosed recesses, as with an *a*, are difficult to smooth. The bent 21 sweep 5/16-inch (8 mm) chisel (or narrower) can be useful in this instance.

Lowering Surfaces

Lower the surfaces of the letters. This produces a snappy—nearly handwritten—overall picture. First use the flat 3 sweep ⅜-inch (10 mm) chisel to cut the lower lines of the letters on which the script is theoretically placed, and then cut in vertically on the edge (see photo). If necessary, use a stop line before lowering the surfaces.

Tips & Tricks

◆ The background plays an important role with relief lettering. Thus, the guideline should be drawn with special care and the background should be lowered to a uniform depth.

◆ If reducing and refining the background doesn't go as hoped, small defects can be disguised by treating the surface. The best option for patterning the background is stippling (see page 57).

◆ A bent chisel is easier to use than a straight one for cutting the bottom of the letters.

◆ To prevent splitting of the wood while lowering the surface, it is best to work down to the depth alternately and gradually from the top and the sides.

◆ If necessary, use fine sandpaper to remove any remaining marks.

◆ Examples of very low relief include the embossing of coins and medals. If you inspect these closely from the top and the side, you will see that the designs are just a fraction of a millimeter high, and yet they still create a strong three-dimensional impression.

◆ For better visibility, the background to be removed can be shaded with pencil.

Note

◆ Basically any physical subject can be carved in low relief. However, humans and animals are quite complex because of their body and facial shapes, and are not recommended for beginners.

LOW RELIEF

We will carve a daisy with two leaves as an example of low relief. The daisy stands out approximately ³/₈ inch (1 cm) from the background, but even this relatively low depth provides an interesting light-and-dark sculptural effect by casting shadows. The three-dimensional appearance is accomplished by the lowered surface surrounding the flower and the naturalistic composition of the surface.

Step-by-Step Instructions

1 Lowering the Background

Transfer the pattern for the daisy on page 123 onto the sawn 1-inch (2.5 cm) board and clamp the wood down firmly. Use the 10 sweep ¼-inch (6 mm) gouge across the grain to cut two stop lines (1). Then use the same chisel to cut the area between the subject and the previously drawn border down to a depth of approximately ³/₈ inch (1 cm) (2). Leave approximately ³/₈ inch (1 cm) around the subject to prevent formation of any small splits.

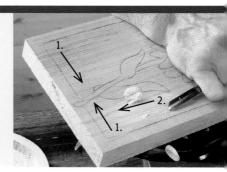

2 Opening Up the Flower

Cut the bottom to a maximum of approximately ½ inch (1.3 cm) and work up to the subject and the border. To speed things up, you can use a larger gouge on the flat part, such as an 11 sweep ¾-inch (19 mm). Using the sculptor's mallet will produce very precise work.

3 Cutting the Edges Straight Down and Forming the Leaves

Now cut down vertically around the blocky subject and the edge. In tight places, corners, and edges use the 45° / ³/₁₆-inch (5 mm) V-gouge, and on straight or rounded surfaces use the 7 sweep ³/₈-inch (10 mm) medium gouge. Use the 3 sweep ³/₈-inch (10 mm) shallow gouge to make a crisp, vertical edge around the two leaves on the stem.

4 Shaping the Center of the Flower

Use the 5 sweep ½-inch (13 mm) shallow gouge to curve the surface of the flower in toward the center. Use a curved 16 sweep ⁵/₈-inch (16 mm) medium gouge to make the resulting corona in the center of the flower even more three-dimensional (see illustration). Round off the center of the flower evenly with a 5 sweep ½-inch (13 mm) medium gouge.

5 Lowering the Flower Petals

Using the same shallow gouge, lower the flower petals outward toward the edge and round them for a three-dimensional effect. Work from the highest point on the leaves toward the edge, taking off very little wood. The edges of the flower should stand up approximately 3/16- to 5/16-inch (5 to 8 mm).

6 Lowering the Leaves

Give the leaves a sweeping shape with the shallow gouge or the curved gouge, and use the 16 sweep 5/8-inch (16 mm) medium gouge to give the stem a uniform roundness. Pay close attention to the wood grain to avoid splintering.

7 Final Shaping of Petals

A natural look is achieved by setting the individual petals apart from one another with the 45° / 3/16-inch (5 mm) V-gouge and further lowering them in parts. Individual sweeping and irregular grooves strengthen the lifelike impression.

8 Cross-Section of the Low Relief

This cross-section again reveals how an astonishingly sculptural feel can be produced by even shallow depth. Initially the daisy stands up only approximately 9/16-inch (14 mm), and subsequently the edges, in particular, are lowered considerably. With its sculptural configuration, the subject remains visually connected to the background at all places.

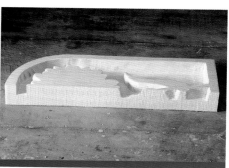

Note

◆ Different heights within the subject often require a change in the direction of cut to avoid cutting against the grain.

Tips & Tricks

◆ For your first projects, use basswood, Eastern white pine, or Swiss stone pine. It takes advanced skill to work hardwoods with lots of grain.

Note

◆ In comparison to the cross-section of the low relief on the bottom of page 35, the daisy done in high relief (before under-cutting) clearly shows the difference in the spatial depth. The lowered border puts the subject even more clearly into the fore-ground. The subse-quent undercutting of the interstices that are visible from the side, but not the front, makes the subject appear higher and more natural.

Tips & Tricks

◆ Cut down only as far as you can and still produce a smooth surface.

◆ Reproducing natural perspective requires a clear vision and a bit of practice to create a three-dimensional, realistic depiction through deliberate undercut-ting and background removal.

HIGH RELIEF

The transition from low to high relief requires a few additional considerations. The subjects now stand higher over the background, so more wood must be removed. With increased height the shapes and the angle of view also change. The objects become noticeably more realistic and in many places they appear to be standing free of the background.

Step-by-Step Instructions

1 Lowering the Background

Transfer the daisy pattern from page 123 to the sawn 2-inch (5.1 cm) board and clamp the board down securely. As with the low relief, remove the wood surrounding the daisy with the 10 sweep ¼-inch (6 mm) gouge and the V-gouge. First cut the background down to a little less than ⅝-inch (1.6 cm), then work the surface down smoothly to a little more than 1 inch (2.5 cm). Smooth the bottom with the 21 sweep ⁵⁄₁₆-inch (8 mm) bent chisel.

2 Adjusting the Height of the Frame

Use a 5 sweep ½-inch (13 mm) shallow gouge to cut the frame down to a height of approximately ⅜-inch (1 cm). Pay attention to the direction of the grain so the wood doesn't splinter. Change the direction of the cut if necessary (see page 21, How Wood Grain Affects the Cut).

3 Shaping the Leaves and the Stem

Lower the stem and the leaves approximately ⁹⁄₁₆-inch (1.4 cm) with the same shallow gouge. Roughly shape the leaves and the stem; the three parts (stem and two leaves) should be clearly set apart by dividing lines (use the shallow gouge for these, too). The stem should have a uniform curve and end at the lowered frame around the subject.

4 Flattening the Flower

Lower the flower significantly toward the right and the outside; ultimately the lowered outside edge should have a height of approximately ⅜-inch (1 cm). This produces the spatial effect of a flower that leans toward the side. Once again remove the wood with the 5 sweep ½-inch (13 mm) shallow gouge.

Carving Out the Center of the Flower

5 Cut from the petals into the center using the 5 sweep ½-inch (13 mm) shallow gouge. Shape the center of the flower so it is rounded and domed, with a slight indentation in the middle, and stands out from the background. It is then approximately 1 inch (2.5 cm) lower than the outer rim of the flower.

Sculpting the Leaves in Three Dimensions

6 Give the stem and the leaves a realistic shape. Lower the stem further and shape the upper leaf so that it curves over the stem. Divide the lower leaf from the stem with a deliberate, vertical cut and lower it a bit from the stem. Give the outer part of the leaf some sweep. Check the tops and the edges of the flower, stem, and leaves for smooth transitions and perfect them if necessary. Good choices for these cuts are the 5 sweep ⅝-inch (16 mm), 5 sweep ½-inch (13 mm), and 7 sweep ⅜-inch (10 mm).

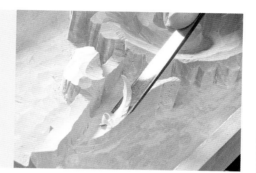

Sculpting the Flower in Three Dimensions

7 Start cutting in around the flower. The petals should be approximately ¼-inch (6 mm) tall. As an aid a parallel guideline can be drawn approximately ¼ inch (6 mm) from the top edge of the flower. Set the 5 sweep ½-inch (13 mm) shallow gouge on this line, and cut downward at an angle to approximately ⅛-inch (3 mm) above the bottom to free up the form, petal by petal, into a wreath shape.

Cutting In around the Flower

8 Remove the remaining wood chips that are not yet completely severed. Use the 11 sweep ¾-inch (19 mm) U-gouge at right angles to the chips and cut them off deliberately. As the depth increases, change to the 10 sweep ⅜-inch (10 mm) and 11 sweep 1/16-inch (2 mm) sweeps. Don't cut into the bottom as you do this, for the previously established depth must be preserved. In removing the remaining chips, the gouge must be guided parallel to the bottom.

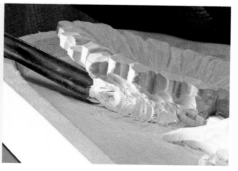

Undercutting the Flower

9 As the depth increases, change to the 16 sweep ⅝-inch (16 mm) curved chisel and cleanly cut out the bottom using an 11 sweep 1/16-inch (2 mm) U-gouge and smooth it if necessary. Once the desired depth is reached, shape the surface of the flower to appear natural, as in the low relief exercise, or according to preference.

Tips & Tricks

◆ You can use a depth gauge to see if you have lowered the background to a uniform depth. You can easily make a depth gauge yourself, using a thin, fairly long piece of wood (approximately 3/32 inch thick [2 to 3 mm]) with a thin nail driven through it. Place the depth gauge over the lowered background and secure the nail in the position that corresponds to the desired depth of your relief. Now place the depth gauge with the nail on various places in the background and adjust the depth as needed.

◆ The undercutting in this example is so deep that a thumb fits between the bottom and the underside of the flower.

CELTIC KNOT BOOKENDS

Transfer the design in accordance with the pattern onto the basswood block and clamp it down. Use the 10 sweep ¼-inch (6 mm) U-gouge to lower the area around the knot by approximately 2 inches (5.1 cm). Cut in vertically around the design with a 3 sweep ³/₁₆-inch (5 mm) shallow gouge and smooth the bottom. Lower all the underlying sections of band (see also Lettering, page 33). Finally, curve the top surface of the subject using the shallow gouge.

SIZE
Approximately
3½ inches (9 cm)

MATERIAL
- Basswood blocks,
  approximately 2¼ x
  3½ x 2 inches (5.7 x 9
  x 5.1 cm)

CARVING TOOLS
- Shallow Gouge:
  3 sweep ³/₁₆-inch (5 mm)
- U-gouge: 10 sweep
  ¼-inch (6 mm)

PATTERN
Page 123

VARIANT
Page 59

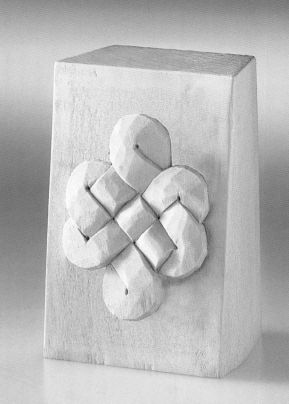

PROJECT IDEAS

SIZE
Approximately 6¼ x 10¼
inches (15.9 cm x 26 cm)

MATERIAL
- Basswood board, approximately 6¼ x 10¼ x 1 inches
  (15.9 cm x 26 cm x 2.5 cm)
  thick

CARVING TOOLS
- Shallow gouge:
  5 sweep ½-inch (13 mm)
- U-gouges:
  7 sweep ³/₈-inch (10 mm),
  16 sweep ⁵/₈-inch (16 mm),
  9 sweep ⁵/₁₆-inch (8 mm),
  18 sweep ½-inch (13 mm),
  10 sweep ¼-inch (6 mm),
  10 sweep ³/₈-inch (10 mm),
  11 sweep ¾-inch (19 mm),
  and 20 sweep ³/₈-inch (10 mm)

PATTERN
Page 123

DECORATIVE ORNAMENT

Transfer the lines of the subje to the wood in accordance wi the pattern, and mark the ba ground depth ³/₈ inch (1 cm) on all four sides. Use 5 swee ½-inch (13 mm) and 18 swee ½-inch (13 mm) to work the various depths and curved sections out to the edge. Use the U-gouges and shallow gouges to create the details of the recesses and fillets.

Notes

- With this design you have to take into account the continuous changing wood grain. Always cu with the grain to avoid breaking tops of the ridges.

A SAYING CARVED IN RELIEF

...nsfer the text to the board ...d remove the wood around it ... a depth of approximately ¹/₈ ...h (3 mm), to a distance of ...proximately ¹/₈ inch (3 mm) ...m the text. This distance is ...cessary so that the letters can ...den by approximately 10° to ... toward the background and ...s appear more solidly ...ounded. The letters are sepa-...ed and shaped using the ...gouge and U-gouges.

SIZE
Approximately 7¹/₂ x 12 inches (19 cm x 30.5 cm)

MATERIAL
- Basswood board, Approximately 7¹/₂ x 12 x 1 inches (19 x 30.5 x 2.5 cm)

CARVING TOOLS
- Shallow gouge: 3 sweep ³/₁₆-inch (5 mm)
- U-gouges: 10 sweep ¹/₄-inch (6 mm) and 11 sweep ¹/₁₆-inch (2 mm)
- V-gouge: 45° / ³/₁₆-inch (5 mm)

PATTERN
Page 123

RELIEF CARVING

SIZE
Approximately 10 inches (25.4 cm)

MATERIAL
FOR EACH RELIEF
- Swiss stone pine or Eastern white pine board, approximately 10 x 12 inches (25.4 x 30.5 cm), 1 to 2 inches (2.5 to 5.1 cm) thick

CARVING TOOLS
- Bent chisel: 21 sweep ⁵/₁₆-inch (8 mm)
- Shallow sweep gouges: 3 sweep ³/₈-inch (10 mm), 5 sweep ⁵/₁₆-inch (8 mm), and 5 sweep ¹/₂-inch (13 mm)
- Medium sweep gouges: 7 sweep ³/₈-inch (10 mm) and 16 sweep ⁵/₈-inch (16 mm)
- U-gouges: 10 sweep ¹/₄-inch (6 mm), 10 sweep ³/₈-inch (10 mm), 11 sweep ¹/₁₆-inch (2 mm), and 11 sweep ³/₄-inch (19 mm)
- V-gouge: 45° / ³/₁₆-inch (5 mm)

PATTERN
Page 123

DAISY IN HIGH AND LOW RELIEF

Both relief carvings are done as described on pages 23 to 27. The petals and the leaves are sculpted individually. Cut in the decorative lines and natural structures with a V-gouge.

Tips & Tricks

- Depending on the thickness of the piece of wood, different three-dimensional effects can be created with low and high relief carving. With low relief the flower can be carved so that the contours are merely hinted at above the background.

4 SCULPTURAL CARVING

Notes

◆ In general, sculptural carving involves freestanding, three-dimensional objects that present a different appearance from varying points of view. While relief work, discussed in the previous chapter, can also have a three-dimensional, solid structure and a sculptural quality, it is not freestanding in space because of the unbreakable connection with the flat background. This basic definition is something to keep in mind when you carve or create sculptures.

One effective and wood-saving way to develop a feel for harmonious proportions and shapes is to work with modeling clay. The human figure is the greatest challenge for every wood carver, and working with clay lets you experiment in getting the figure right. It's not always possible to correct a sculptural carving once too much wood has been removed. Clay is also helpful in determining the proper wall thickness when carving bowls. Modeling clay can be bought cheaply in hobby shops.

An old saying among woodcarvers is that every sculpture is already present inside the wood; the task of the sculptor is to cut away the parts that don't belong. This requires not only a good ability to visualize in three dimensions, but—especially when carving figures—a feel for proportion. One good way to learn the basics of sculptural carving is to start with plain bowls and simple figures that lack facial features and other challenging details.

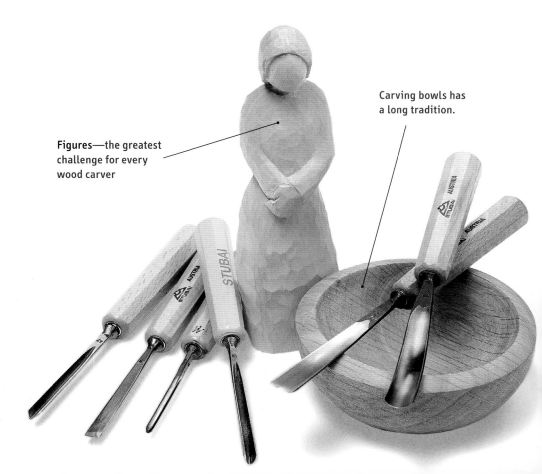

Figures—the greatest challenge for every wood carver

Carving bowls has a long tradition.

CARVING BOWLS

Bowls have been used by humans for thousands of years for many purposes. As storage containers, they tend to be plain, thick-walled, and sturdy. As decorative items, they can be thin-walled, light, and delicate. In the following step-by-step tutorial, a small, round bowl with a thick wall will be carved from durable, highly figured oak.

Step-by-Step Instructions

Marking the Inside Diameter

1 Use a compass (or the circle template on page 127) to draw the inside and outside diameters, with radii of 2 inches (5.1 cm) and 2½ inches (6.4 cm), respectively, onto the clamped-down 2-inch-thick (5.1 cm) rough-sawn wood of the appropriate size; here the diameter is approximately 5¼ inches (13.3 cm). The markings are easy to see on the wood.

Carving Out the Inside of the Bowl

2 To lay out the inside of the bowl, start the hollowing with the 5 sweep ½-inch (13 mm) shallow gouge. Keep a distance of approximately ³⁄₈-inch (1 cm) from the previously scribed inner edge, always cutting inward toward the center. During these first cuts you can get used to the special qualities and the hardness of the oak.

Working on the Rim

3 Circumscribe the outer rim along the circular line using the shallow chisel with a 5 sweep ½-inch (13 mm). Cut down vertically approximately ³⁄₄ inch (1.9 cm) from the surface. This produces the outer rim. Drawing arrows helps with orientation.

Continuing to Work on the Inside of the Bowl

4 Use the curved 16 sweep ⁵⁄₈-inch (16 mm) shallow gouge to continue deepening the inner curvature of the bowl. Work the inner surface to a maximum depth of approximately 1³⁄₄ inches (4.4 cm), keeping the curvature uniform. Work the curvature into the center of the bowl from the inner wall scribed at the outset.

Carving Bowls continued

Carving Bowls
continued

Tips & Tricks

◆ After carving a few bowls you will quickly develop a feel for the inside and outside shapes and the appropriate thickness of the walls. Then the outer shape can be carved from the outset, followed by contouring the inside.

Note

◆ Carving a bowl by hand is laborious, but it's the best way to get a feel for the hardness of the wood and the direction of the grain. It will also help you do other, more complicated carving projects.

5 Shaping from the Rim to the Bottom

Carve the outer wall down to the bottom using a shallow gouge with a 5 sweep ½-inch (13 mm). Notice: In this direction of carving, the wood may split near the bottom; if this happens, immediately change the direction of the cut, such as from bottom to top, always cutting away from your body.

6 Beveling the Rim

Use the same shallow gouge to slightly bevel the rim toward the outside (approximately 10°). Pay close attention to the grain direction. Rework if the rim is not the same thickness all the way around. Later on it should slant inward and outward.

7 Rounding the Rim and Working on the Bottom

For the bottom, use a compass with a radius set to just over 1½ inches (3.8 cm) to draw a circle around the center of the bottom surface. Use a shallow gouge with a 5½ inch (14 cm) sweep to create the outer contour of the bowl while maintaining a uniform wall thickness. For security, keep the bowl clamped solidly to the work plate. If necessary, use the contour of the pattern on page 127 as a guideline.

8 Refining the Wall

Continue using the 5 sweep ½-inch (13 mm) gouge to work the wall in greater detail. If you are not sure about the thickness of the wall, remove the bowl from the clamp, check the thickness of the wall between thumb and forefinger, and continue working.

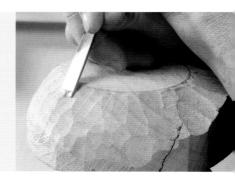

9 Sanding the Surface

Bring out the wood grain through careful sanding, starting with 80 grit and progressing in steps from 100 grit to 180 grit. You can create an attractive contrast by sanding the inside of the bowl very smooth while only slightly smoothing the coarse outer wall.

Carving Figures

Carving figures is considered to be the highest order of carving art. Anyone who begins figure carving and finds satisfaction will soon see potential subjects everywhere. However, the beginner is advised to develop the techniques of figure carving gradually, starting not with figures of complex postures, clothing, or facial expressions, but rather with simple, erect, somewhat stylized shapes, as in the following example.

Step-by-Step Instructions

Preparing the Basic Shape

1 Begin by using the patterns on page 127 as templates. Transfer the frontal outline to the front of the block of wood and saw along the lines. Then transfer the template for the side and do the same, following the lines. In order to secure the blank with screws from the underside, saw the wood so as to create a base approximately ¾ inch (1.9 cm) thick that will later be removed.

Roughing Out the Head

2 Round off the four-sided head using a 3 sweep ³⁄₈-inch (10 mm) shallow gouge on the top half and rough it out. Viewed from above, it should have an oval shape with no straight edges. Carefully smooth any uneven spots.

Shaping from the Head to the Neck

3 In the lower half, rough out a slender transition to the neck. Then use the shallow gouge to round the faceted throat area and remove the sharp ridges. Check your work by setting the figure upright, turning it, and looking for irregular contours.

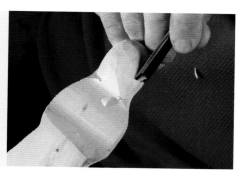

Shaping the Skirt Down to the Floor

4 Use a 5 sweep ½-inch (13 mm) shallow gouge (or narrower) to round off the lower part of the figure and shape it into a skirt. This should produce a uniform oval shape at the bottom seam (the surface on which the figure stands). (See Tips and Tricks.)

Tips & Tricks

◆ Here's how to shape the skirt section described in step 4. As viewed from below, a regularly shaped oval surface should be carved out of the block of wood. To achieve this, remove wood mostly from the edges and less toward the center. At the outer midpoints, which are designated by arrows, no wood is carved away. These arrows can be drawn on the side of the rough blank as guidelines. Now the figure can be set upright, the center of the four sides measured, and vertical lines drawn on them with a pencil.

Between these lines, regular quadrant-like contours are now carved (see sketch).

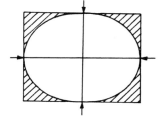

Carving Figures
continued

Carving Figures
continued

Note

◆ The guide for body proportions is useful for getting started in carving figures because the body parts are compact, largely undifferentiated, and hence easier to carve. You can move at your own pace from these simple shapes and postures to add more details, such as hand position and facial expression.

Tips & Tricks

◆ It is easy to create a correct, natural shoulder position with the help of a ruler. Begin by placing the ruler on the side of the figure. By locating the shoulder joint directly behind this imaginary vertical midline (plumb line), the body will not appear too stout.

5 Roughing Out the Arms and Hands

The hands can be shown clasped in front of the body and outlined at hip height in a V shape by using a 10 sweep ¼-inch (6 mm) U-gouge. Carve them farther toward the hips to show the forearms up to the elbows.

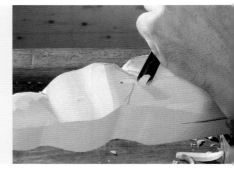

6 Shaping the Skirt and Hips

Keep working on the skirt along the contours already produced, beginning in the center and working toward the hips. Then round the back of the skirt toward the hips. The skirt now should have no sharp edges or irregular contours.

7 Drawing the Arms

Draw the position of the upper and lower arms on the side of the figure. Starting at the shoulder, both parts should be approximately one head height long. A circle approximately one-and-a-half head heights from the top edge of the figure indicates the location of the shoulder joint.

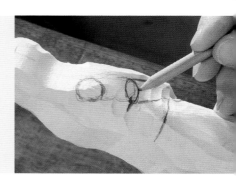

8 Carving the Arm and Elbow

Use a 10 sweep ¼-inch (6 mm) U-gouge to lay out the arms a little more than ½ inch (1.3 cm) wide on both sides from the drawn shoulder joint down to the hands; the arms are slightly bent at the elbows.

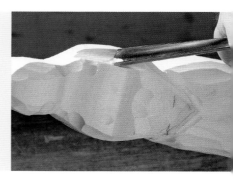

9 Shaping the Rib Cage and Throat

Using the same U-gouge and another with a 7 sweep ³⁄₈-inch (10 mm) configuration, make the throat more slender, round the front, and create a smooth transition to the upper body.

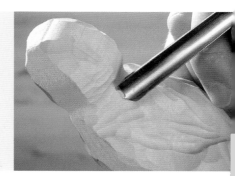

Adding Detail to the Body

10 Make smooth transitions between the individual body parts and gently round the shoulders and proportion the upper arms with even contours. Create the final shape of the head and adjust the throat once again if necessary. Smooth the upper body with a 5 sweep ½-inch (13 mm) shallow sweep gouge.

Setting Off the Arms

11 Now the hair is indicated as a compact area using a 10 sweep ¼-inch (6 mm) U-gouge. Starting at the neck, taper the hair to a narrow pigtail that runs down the center of the back as far as the hips (see step 13). Then round the forearms evenly from where they contact the clothing, continuing down to the hands.

Carving the Hands

12 Now use a V-gouge to carve the hands precisely from the outlines previously created with the U-gouge. Carve the upper hand like a mitten, with the faint suggestion of a thumb. The lower hand is surrounded and visible at the wrist inside the opening of the sleeve.

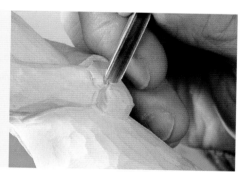

Setting Off the Pigtail

13 Cut around the pigtail with the V-gouge so that it stands up approximately 1/32 inch (1 to 2 mm) from the uniformly rounded back and flows evenly into the hair. It should reveal the curvature of the back when the figure is viewed from above.

Carving the Hairline and Forehead

14 Carve the contours of the hair. Use the V-gouge from the hairline and on both sides of the forehead down to the shoulders. The shape of the hair should flow smoothly when viewed from the side. Round the face using a 3 sweep 3/16-inch (5 mm) shallow gouge to produce a regular, symmetrical face shape when viewed from the front. Keep turning the figure and checking it from different viewpoints.

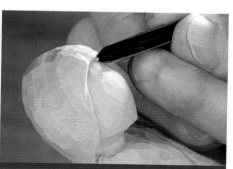

Notes

◆ The wooden manikin based on simplified geometrical shapes that painters use in studying human anatomy may be useful here. The individual wooden parts are connected by joints that move like the human body.

◆ As you draw and carve human figures, compare the relationships of anatomical parts to one another and to the whole; such as the head to body height, the length of the legs to the body, and the upper arms to the lower arms.

BIRD

Saw out the bird according to the pattern on page 125 and clamp the rough blank securely. Use the 7 sweep 3/8-inch (10 mm) shallow gouge to round the shape of the body. Set off the head and the tail with the V-gouge and carve the feathers. Make the head half the width of the body and round it. Use the V-gouge to carve the beak and the eyes.

Note

◆ Wood gradually darkens in sunshine. This has given the bird its warm, reddish-brown color.

SIZE
Approximately 2½ inches (6.4 cm)

MATERIAL
◆ Block of eastern white pine, approximately 4 x 2½ x 2 inches (10.2 x 6.4 x 5.1 cm)

CARVING TOOLS
◆ Carving knife
◆ V-gouge: 45° / 3/16-inch (5 mm)

PATTERN
Page 125

PROJECT IDEAS

SIZE
Approximately 8 inches (20.3 cm)

MATERIAL
◆ Block of basswood, 2½ x 8 x 2 inches (6.4 x 20.3 x 5.1 cm)

CARVING TOOLS
◆ Shallow gouges: 3 sweep 3/16-inch (5 mm), 3 sweep 3/8-inch (10 mm), and 5 sweep ½-inch (13 mm)
◆ Gouge: 10 sweep ¼-inch (6 mm)
◆ V-gouge: 45° / 3/16-inch (5 mm)

PATTERN
Page 127

A SIMPLE FIGURE

Carve the figure as described o pages 43 to 45. See the photos full views of the front and back

Tips & Tricks

◆ If you don't have experience shaping, you should first make figure out of modeling clay. Thi especially useful in practicing t arms and face.

A SHALLOW BOWL

Draw the shape of the bowl onto the board according to the pattern, and saw it out. First rough out the inside with the chisels, then refine the carving and work on the outside and the rim. Finally, sand the whole bowl to your liking.

SIZE
Approximately 7 x 4 x 1½ inches (17.8 x 10.2 x 3.8 cm) tall

MATERIAL
- Plum wood sideboard, approximately 9 x 6 x 1½ inches (22.9 x 15.2 x 3.8 cm) tall

CARVING TOOLS INSIDE OF BOWL
- Shallow gouge: 5 sweep ¾-inch (19 mm)
- Medium gouges: 7 sweep ⅜-inch (10 mm) and 16 sweep ⅝-inch (16 mm)

OUTSIDE OF BOWL
- Shallow Gouge: 4 sweep 1-inch (25 mm)

PATTERN
Page 127

SCULPTURAL CARVING

SIZE
8¼ x 3 x 2¾ inches (21 x 7.6 cm, 7 cm)

MATERIAL
- Quarter-sawn plum wood, radius approximately 4½ x 8¾ inches (11.4 x 22.2 cm)

CARVING TOOLS INSIDE OF BOWL
- Shallow gouge: 3 sweep ⅝-inch (16 mm)
- Medium gouges: 7 sweep ⅜-inch (10 mm) and 16 sweep ⅝-inch (16 mm)

OUTSIDE OF BOWL
- Shallow gouges: 3 sweep ⅝-inch (16 mm) and 4 sweep 1-inch (25 mm)

PATTERN
Page 127

A DEEP BOWL

Create the shape of the bowl from the quarter-sawn trunk according to the pattern. First work on the bottom of what will become the base. Then rough out the inside, carve it neatly, and sand it. Now work on the outer shape, and finally smooth the rim and the outer surface with sandpaper.

Tips & Tricks

- Even a crack in the wood can be worked into the design in an attractive way. This one, for example, can be reworked with a slender woodcarving knife.

5 CARVING ON THE GO

Notes

◆ Carving on the go makes economical use of materials that are free for the taking. Decorations, toys, and useful items can be carved from odd branches and leftover wood scraps.

◆ If you have not yet done any carving, we recommend beginning with woods that are easy to work, such as birch, basswood, and juniper. Many attractive figures can also be carved from willow and corkscrew hazel branches.

With all the carving techniques you learned in chapters 2 through 4, you saw the necessity of clamping the work piece tightly while carving. In this chapter we will show you how to carve small, attractive items without a clamping jig by using only a folding saw and a simple carving knife or a lock-back folding knife.

Children and teenagers especially like working with fresh, fragrant wood that they themselves cut to shape and carve. Think about a "carving party" on the next child's birthday or whenever the kids have some spare time.

On your walks, hikes, or picnics, keep a lookout for branches with intriguing bends, swellings, holes, or forks. You will be amazed at how many pieces of wood already have figures or shapes waiting to be discovered by the alert carver.

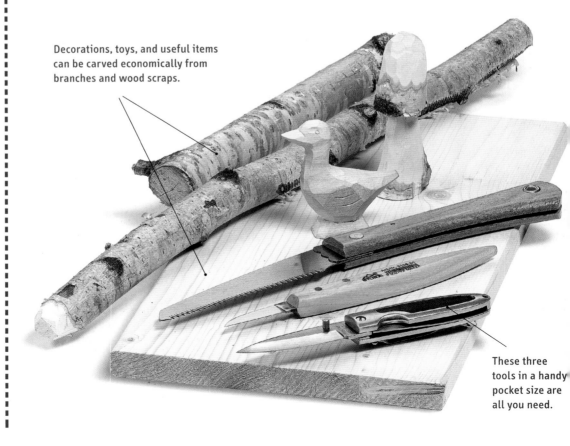

Decorations, toys, and useful items can be carved economically from branches and wood scraps.

These three tools in a handy pocket size are all you need.

OOLS & TECHNIQUES

ools

u can use a handy folding saw (with a locking blade to event injuries) to quickly and easily cut off branches, igs, and small pieces of boards and planks.

stead of a chip carving knife you can also use a pocknife with a locking blade. An ordinary pocketknife is s suited to carving because it can suddenly fold shut en you cut into the wood with the point. Nor do we ommend multi-purpose knives, which are usually ck and awkward.

simple carving knife (or bench knife; also see page 14) really an all-purpose knife with which you can make ts, contours, and neat chips and depressions.

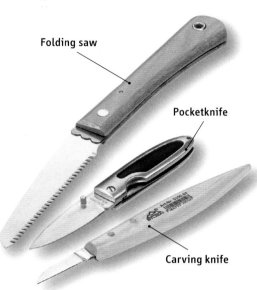

Folding saw

Pocketknife

Carving knife

(also see page 16).

Tips & Tricks

◆ Protect your carving knife and the small folding knife by carrying them in a case or roll when not in use (also see page 16).

◆ Your work will be safer and easier if you sharpen the carving knife and the pocketknife regularly (see pages 18 to 19).

◆ One way to avoid injuries to the thumb with the paring cut is to protect it with several layers of adhesive bandages. Never cut directly toward your thumb, and pull the knife out shortly before it reaches your thumb, as with a fruit peeler.

◆ Before carving decorative bands and the intended pattern, do a sketch first. Note that too much carving in the bark affects its durability, and sections of bark that end in a point tend to chip.

◆ If the ends of a piece of wood are to be worked, the cut must always angle in toward the pith. If the cutting is done outward from the pith, the wood will split near the bark.

ypes of Cut

the preceding chapters you learned that you should cut away from your body whenever possible. This is not vays possible for items you carve while holding by hand, so extra care is called for.

nple shapes and figures can be produced easily with just two types of cut, the push cut and the paring cut. nds and ring-shaped patterns can set off decorations with sharp borders.

sh Cut
t safely away from your body en using this technique. Hold e branch or piece of wood htly and place the blade in nt of the holding hand at a rly shallow angle on the place u intend to cut. The thumb of e other hand supports the back the blade and firmly secures piece of wood being cut. The od is now cut away at the front th a short, forward-prying tion.

Paring Cut
This cut is like the simple cutting movement used to peel an apple or orange. Again, hold the branch or piece of wood firmly (ideally the holding hand should be behind the hand that guides the carving knife), and place the knife at a shallow angle, with the cutting edge facing your body. Make sure the thumb of the hand guiding the knife does not lie on the wood, or you may cut it if the blade slips.

Carving Decorative Bands
Bands (ring-shaped decorations) are carved primarily for decorating objects made from branches. Hold the branch or section of branch tightly with one hand. Use the carving knife to cut two parallel grooves at the desired distance from each other and down into the sapwood. Then "pry out" the bark and the phloem inside this circular cut with careful push cuts. The incised grooves keep the knife from slipping beyond the limit.

Tips & Tricks

◆ For a first attempt, cut off a piece of birch branch a little over 1 inch (2.5 cm) thick and approximately 20 inches (50.8 cm) long. For ease in holding, first carve the mushroom on the wood and cut it off the branch at the end.

◆ Support the tip of the stick on a piece of wood or a log. Carve away from your body toward the base to prevent injury.

◆ You can also use the paring cut with this subject. With fairly thick branches, in fact, the paring cut toward the thumb is the best way to round the head of the mushroom.

Carving Branches

This decorative mushroom is made from a birch branch. While you can use any type of wood, freshly cut woods are easier to carve because of their higher water content. Choose branches o sections with no inner growths or branching. A uniform fiber structure will make it easier for you to get the feel of carving.

Step-by-Step Instructions

Sawing out the Head of the Mushroom

Cut a piece from a birch branch with an approximate diameter of 1 inch (2.5 cm). For the top of the mushroom, use the handsaw to cut all the way around the bark to a depth of approximately $3/16$ inch (5 mm), approximately $1\frac{1}{2}$ inches (3.8 cm) from the end.

1

Rounding the Head of the Mushroom

Start rounding approximately 1 inch (2.5 cm) from this end using a push cut. Approximately $3/8$ inch (1 cm) of bark remains all the way around for the rim of the cap. Use very fine push cuts to work the tip and round it off smoothly.

2

Carving the Base of the Stem

Taper the stem to the sawn groove under the mushroom cap; use the push cut to work down to a depth of approximately $5/16$ inch (8 mm).

3

Shaping the Stem

If you want to, leave a little bark at the end of the stem, or carve it all off. A nice look is produced when the edge of the remaining bark is scalloped.

4

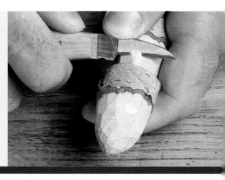

Carving with Wood Scraps

As with branches, many attractive items can be carved from simple scraps of boards and planks. Small figures such as animals are easy to make once the basic shape or rough blank is cut out with a coping saw. Here, too, a sharp folding knife is adequate for the work.

Step-by-Step Instructions

Cutting out a Rough Blank

1 Transfer the pattern for the figure (see page 127) to the wood with the aid of a cardboard template and cut out the subject with a coping saw. Since the figure is relatively compact, the paring cut is most useful.

Carving the Base

2 Evenly taper the base below the goose toward the top on all sides. Carve the base to a depth of approximately ¼ inch (6 mm) at the narrowest point, right under the belly.

Shaping the Body

3 Round the belly toward the base with the paring cut. You will be cutting against the grain, so use multiple thin cuts. Round the goose's back and taper it to a point at the tail. Then round the neck; the lower portion should be approximately ³/₈ inch (1 cm) thick.

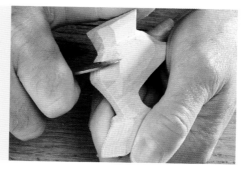

Shaping the Head

4 Now shape the goose's head. It should be about ⁵/₃₂ inch (4 mm) broader than the throat. Work the beak down to a point and carefully round the top of the head.

To finish up, carve the eyes (see page 52).

Tips & Tricks

◆ A cardboard template makes it easy to position the subject on scrap wood.

◆ You can also carve the figure by simply drawing the outlines onto the wood and carving the body out of the wood. In this case it's a good idea also to draw the outlines for a front or rear view (see also page 23, "Using Photos as Patterns").

MUSHROOMS

Make mushrooms from branches of different lengths and thicknesses as described on page 50. The mushrooms look very good when the bark is totally removed from the stems.

Tips & Tricks

◆ Good woods for carving mushrooms include boxwood, juniper, black elder, and apple.

SIZE
Approximately 2 to 4½ inches (5.1 to 27.9 cm)

MATERIAL
◆ Birch or hazel wood branch

CARVING CHISELS AND TOOLS
◆ Folding handsaw
◆ Chip carving knife or folding knife

PROJECT IDEAS

SIZE
Approximately 3 inches (9.6 cm)

MATERIAL
◆ Basswood block, approximately 3 x 2⅞ x 1¼ inches (7.6 x 7.3 x 3.2 cm)

CARVING TOOLS
◆ Chip carving knife or folding knife

PATTERN
Page 127

GOOSE

Carve the goose as described in the Workshop on page 51. Use the chip carving knife or the folding knife to cut two or three short grooves into each side to suggest the plumage. Carve in the eyes as short, narrow slits.

Tips & Tricks

◆ It's easier to carve this subject if you hold it by a base approximately 3 inches (7.6 cm) long. Either cut this out at the same time you saw out the outline or glue a round piece of wood on the previously drilled base and saw it off when you're finished. You can also make the eyes with a fine U-gouge.

FOND HEARTS

Transfer the pattern for a pair of hearts to the wood and saw out the shape along the outline with a scroll saw. For the large hearts, use the chip carving knife to round the wood to the mid-point of its thickness. Begin at the edges of both short sides and carve into the center of the shape. If necessary, draw a vertical centerline. The hearts remain flat on the back. For the small hearts, the figures are completely rounded. Start the carving on the top and round the shape on both sides to the center of the wood thickness.

SIZE
Large hearts: approximately 6 x 3 x 2 inches (15.2 x 7.6 x 5.1 cm)

Small hearts: approximately 4 x 2¾ x 1½ inches (10.2 x 7 x 3.8 cm)

MATERIAL
- Large hearts: block of Swiss stone pine (or equivalent), 6 x 3 x 2 inches (15.2 x 7.6 x 5.1 cm)
- Small hearts: 4 x 2¾ x 1½ inches (10.2 x 7 x 3.8 cm)

CARVING TOOLS
- Chip carving knife or folding knife

PATTERN
Page 127

CARVING ON THE GO

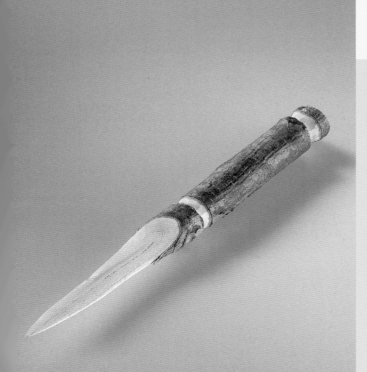

LENGTH
Approximately 9 inches (22.9 cm)

MATERIAL
- Hazelwood branch, approximately ¾ inch (1.9 cm) in diameter

TOOLS
- Folding handsaw
- Chip carving knife or folding knife

PATTERN
Page 127

LETTER OPENER

Notch around a 9-inch-long (22.9 cm) branch to stop the cuts. Flatten out the cuts with the knife. To reduce the risk of injury, slightly round the cutting edge and the point. Round the end with a push cut, and decorate it with a beveled ring.

Tips & Tricks

- Ripples in the wood grain make it difficult to form a smooth blade. Finish it carefully with sandpaper if necessary.

The Basic Equipment

For surface work, you should keep the following materials and tools handy:

- Primer
- Paint brushes in various sizes
- Varnish brush
- Water glass
- An old plate or mixing palette
- Lint-free rags or paper towels
- Sponge
- Cotton Swabs

In the previous chapters you learned how to choose the right wood for your carving project and how to use tools and chisels properly. You also saw that the carvings have their own decorative quality even without surface treatments. In this chapter, however, we hope to persuade you that a few treatment techniques can greatly enhance the visual qualities of the wood. You will learn some of the most familiar and yet useful approaches including painting, scumbling, varnishing, oiling, and stippling.

You will also see that not every treatment is appropriate for every design or type of wood. The more you experiment with the individual properties of the wood and the items you carve, the more confidence you will gain in selecting the appropriate surface treatment.

Watercolors for a bright finish

Small piece of sponge can be used to create neat color effects

Oils bring out the wood grain.

Stippling punches help create exciting surfaces.

Varnishes provide shee

Painting

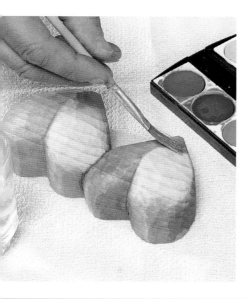

Painting is the commonest surface treatment. The color you choose for painting depends on both the desired visual effect and how the item will be used. You can create an attractive surface with simple watercolors, acrylics, or tinting paints, and certainly with the more expensive oils. The carved item must first be finished cleanly, since painting over rough places or protruding fibers will complicate the final finish, especially if several colors come into contact with one another. Paints can either cover the surface completely or act like a glaze. In painting with a glaze, the color is thinned with water (in a proportion of about 1:10) and brushed on in the direction of the wood grain. The wood structure remains visible after painting and thus provides additional visual interest.

Scumbling

This technique is especially suited to items that have a rather coarse surface. In scumbling, a second color is applied to a surface that has already been painted and allowed to dry. This creates accents such as shading or marbling. In applying the second color, a small, relatively stiff sponge is used. Color is applied sparingly so that it does not collect in depressions but coats primarily the projecting edges. Take as little color as possible into the sponge, and if necessary wipe the sponge on a paper towel before application. Rub the sponge over the carved item, taking care not to press down too firmly.

Varnishing

coat of varnish protects your carved item from dents, atches, and moisture and gives it a unified, waterproof rface. For indoor items you can use commercially availle clear varnish, which comes in matte, semi-gloss, d gloss finishes. It's best to thin the varnish first, then ply it sparingly with either a brush or spray gun. Too ich varnish can flow into unsightly runs. You can so varnish items that have already been painted and owed to dry.

Tips & Tricks

◆ You should have several paint brushes on hand, preferably one for each color. This avoids dirtying a light color with a darker one when you change colors.

◆ Instead of clear lacquer, you can also use hairspray to seal your item and give it some gloss. The spray should be applied from a distance of at least 8 inches (20.3 cm) in regular, small spurts. Keep checking the distance to keep too much varnish from reaching the surface of the wood at one time. If the varnish runs into unattractive trails, the only way to remove it is by sanding.

◆ When applying a glazed finish, you should avoid using white, since this color usually appears gray and unattractive as finish, and it is seldom possible to correct a glazed paint job. It's best to practice this technique on scrap wood before you begin to decorate your carved item.

Tips & Tricks

◆ In addition to oil, paste wax, beeswax, and floor polish can also be used to darken the wood and highlight the grain. Follow carefully the directions on the packaging; some of these products may combust spontaneously.

◆ If certain areas of a burned surface lighten too much when you brush them, you will need to burn these areas again and repeat the brushing.

Oiling

Treating wood with common vegetable oils, a technique known as *priming*, darkens the surface and highlights the grain in a short time. Apply the oil with a soft brush of artificial hairs or swabs of cotton wrapped with cloth.

After application, wipe off excess oil with a soft rag; otherwise the surface will remain sticky instead of drying. To protect the underlying surface, place the bowl on a cloth or a napkin for a couple of days and let it dry thoroughly.

Burning

An interesting surface can be created by burning wood with a blowtorch and subsequently scouring it with a brass bristle brush. Virtually any type of wood can be burned, but the best results are achieved with evergreens, such as spruce and pine, because of their appealing grain. Since the soft early wood and the hard late wood of the annual rings burn at different rates, the process yields attractive color contrasts.

The burning must be done on a fireproof outdoor surface, such as a paved walkway.

Place the carved item on a paving block or brick. Make sure that the stone is set firmly in place and that you can begin burning the lower edge of the wood; then proceed to burn the entire surface. Before beginning, note the manufacture instructions and safety precautions. Brush the burned, cooled surface with the brass bristle brush in the direction the grain (do not use a steel wire brush, which is too hard). Make sure to wear work gloves and a dust mask.

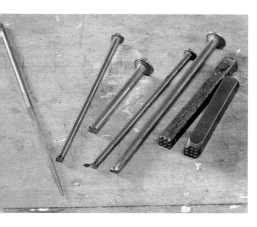

Stippling

Stippling is a decorative technique that has been used for thousands of years to decorate wood, leather, precious metals, and other materials with patterns of points or dots. In stippling on wood, the dots are punched (or *stippled*) into the wood surface as lines and patterns. Punches, available in various sizes and shapes, are styluses made of tool steel and filed into various profiles on the end. These profiles are pounded into the wood with a hammer or a mallet to create patterns.

To get started, place the punch at a right angle to the wood being worked and strike it on the head with a hammer. As you strike, keep the punch moving over the surface of the wood. Hold the shaft of the punch firmly and support your hand by placing the little finger on the work piece. The impressions in the wood should all be the same depth. Avoid striking the punch too hard, as this can splinter the wood.

Making Your Own Punches
To make your own punches, you need thick, steel nails (with the points filed flat) or round steel rods and a file. Clamp the rod in a vise or hold it tightly against the work surface. Now file cross-shaped or triangular patterns on the flattened end.

Tips & Tricks

◆ It's best to practice with punches that have simple shapes. The more elaborate the shapes, the more expensive the tools and the harder it is to correct mistakes. When you buy stippling punches, also note the extent to which various shapes can be blended into a new pattern.

AN OILED BOWL

Carve the bowl as described on pages 41-42 and coat the surface with vegetable oil. If you want a darker color, apply another coat of oil after the first one is dry.

SIZE
Approximately 5 inches (12.7 cm) in diameter and 2 inches (5.1 cm) tall

MATERIAL AND CARVING TOOLS
◆ Bowl; see pages 41-42

ALSO NEEDED
◆ Vegetable oil

PATTERN
Page 127

PROJECT IDEAS

SIZE
Approximately 6 x 3 x 2 inches (15.2 x 7.6 x 5.1 cm)

MATERIAL AND CARVING TOOLS
◆ Large hearts, see top of page 53

ALSO NEEDED
◆ Red and blue watercolors

PATTERN
Page 127

HEARTS IN TWO COLORS

Carve the hearts, then paint the heart on the right using thinned watercolor in transparent red. L the paint dry thoroughly and then paint the heart on the left in blue.

Tips & Tricks

◆ The hearts become truly stri ing with a solid coat of acrylic paint and a clear, glossy varnis sealer. Or, try two different shades of red.

STIPPLED BOOKENDS

Carve the knot design as described on page 38. Measure out a border approximately ¼ inch (6 mm) along all four sides. Use a sharp stippling punch or nail, as described on page 57, to punch in a uniform background. Because of the narrow, sometimes pointed surfaces, only a small tool can be used for this.

SIZE
Approximately 3½ inches (8.9 cm)

MATERIALS AND CARVING TOOLS
◆ Celtic Knot Bookends, see top of page 38

ALSO NEEDED
◆ Pointed stippling punch or nail
◆ Hammer

PATTERN
Page 123

VARIATION
Page 38

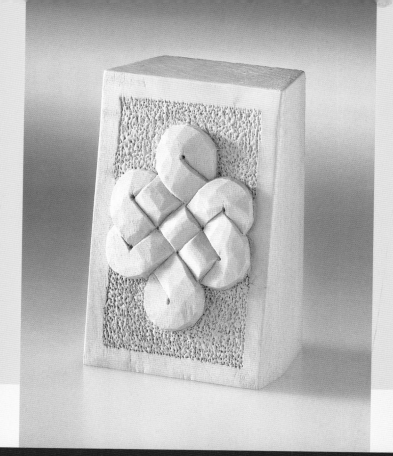

SURFACE TREATMENT

SIZE
Approximately 6 x 3 x 2 inches (15.2 x 7.6 x 5.1 cm)

MATERIALS AND CARVING TOOLS
◆ Large Hearts; see top of page 53

ALSO NEEDED
◆ Red and blue watercolors
◆ Firm sponge

PATTERN
Page 126

HEARTS WITH A MARBLED EFFECT

Carve the heart pattern as described at the top of page 53 for the small hearts. Paint with red watercolor and let dry thoroughly. Use a firm sponge, slightly moistened with blue paint, to rub the color onto the heart.

Tips & Tricks

◆ Scumbling with a piece of leather moistened with paint also works very well. Glue a strip of leather, rough side up, to a conveniently shaped piece of wood. Use a brush to apply some paint to the leather and rub it over the carved surface.

59

APPEALING IDEAS FOR THE HOME

DECORATIONS FOR OUTDOORS

PROJECTS THROUGH THE YEAR

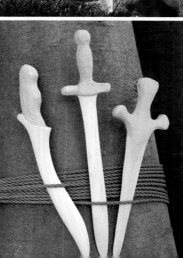

POPULAR CARVING DESIGNS FOR KIDS

PROJECT IDEAS

Always an Appropriate Idea

In the Project Ideas section you will find more than fifty carving projects for house and yard, versatile ideas for all seasons. There is also an extra chapter with simple, neat ideas for children.

If something strikes you as difficult, simply flip back to the Workshop and take another look at the explanation of the appropriate technique.

Practical Materials Lists

Every Project Idea includes a list with information on the appropriate wood and carving chisels. All items in this section can be fashioned using the basic chisels presented in the Workshop on page 17. The materials list also specifies how large each item is (the information on the patterns and plans, starting on page 122, refers to these sizes). The information on sizes should be taken only as a suggestion; feel free to make the selected subject larger or smaller. Just be aware that you may have to change the selection of carving tools.

Tips and Tricks for Success

As in the previous chapters, you will find many tips, tricks, and important notes based on our experiences. As you do your own carving you will have your own experiences and insights. We recommend that you write these down and create your own list of Tips and Tricks. You will see that with a little diligence and practice you will make quick progress.

Notes

◆ The basic skills described in the previous chapters were designed for the completion of particular projects and will not be described further. However, note the page references for these skills so you can refer to them quickly.

◆ With the exception of the carving chisels, the tools mentioned in the Workshop as basic equipment, along with the materials and the drills to make holes for clamping in the vise, are not listed here.

The items in the Project Ideas are divided into the following degrees of difficulty:

   ⟳ **simple**
  ⟳⟳ **a bit more difficult**
 ⟳⟳⟳ **demanding**

APPEALING IDEAS
FOR THE HOME

FLORAL PLATE

Transfer the pattern to the plate. If necessary, separate paper flowers with scissors so that the pattern fits the ~ved surface.

Use a V-gouge to cut along the transferred outlines. Let the s thin on the ends toward the leaves. Go over the veins in leaves with the V-gouge.

Cut in around the center of each flower using a U-gouge and a medium-sweep gouge to scoop out the flower petals in a shape and arch inward toward the center of the flowers.

Carefully round off the cylindrical centers of the flowers n a shallow sweep gouge (see page 34).

Use the V-gouge to structure the leaves and the centers of flowers, either as pictured or as you desire (see page 35).

Color the pattern, for example, by using red on the flower als, yellow on the center of the fl,owers, and green on the es. Note: At first, work only with highly diluted watercolors the flowers and leaves; if desired, use a second coat to ken.

If necessary, smooth the surface with very fine sandpaper. makes the color in the depressions appear more intense the structure of the wood more visible.

DEGREE OF DIFFICULTY
◔◔

SIZE
Approximately 11 inches (27.9 cm) in diameter

MATERIALS
- Shallow dish made from boxwood or maple, 11 inches (27.9 cm) in diameter
- Red, yellow, and green watercolors
- Small brush

CARVING TOOLS
- Shallow gouge:
  3 sweep $^3/_{16}$-inch (5 mm)
- Medium gouges:
  5 sweep $^5/_{16}$-inch (8 mm)
  and 7 sweep $^3/_8$-inch (10 mm)
- V-gouge: 45° / $^3/_{16}$-inch (5 mm)

PATTERN
Page 128

Tips & Tricks

◆ Depending on the size of the plate, you may want to enlarge or reduce the design using a photocopier. You can also use individual elements of the flower pattern or cover the entire plate with them.

◆ To use the dish as a storage container it should first be varnished (flat varnish looks best).

◆ For durability, wooden dishes are usually made from hard woods such as maple, which is difficult to carve. You can find them in most craft supply stores or online.

PAISLEY WALL PLAQUES

Tips & Tricks

◆ Wood soaks up more oil and paint on the vertical sides of recesses. For an even paint job, use highly diluted oil paint in such places.

DEGREE OF DIFFICULTY
◯◯

SIZE
Approximately 8 x 10 inches (20.3 cm x 25.4 cm)

MATERIALS PER WALL HANGING
- Boxwood board approximately 8 x 10 inches (20.3 x 25.4 cm), 1 inch or more (2.5 cm) thick
- Dark red, medium red, orange, green, dark blue, light blue, and ocher oil paints
- Linseed oil
- Various brushes

CARVING TOOLS
- Chisels: 21 sweep ⁵/₁₆-inch (8 mm) and 2 sweep ³/₈-inch (10 mm)
- Shallow gouges: 3 sweep ³/₈-inch (10 mm) and 5 sweep ½-inch (13 mm)
- Medium sweep gouges: 7 sweep ³/₈-inch (10 mm) and 16 sweep ⁵/₈-inch (16 mm)
- U-gouges: 10 sweep ¼-inch (6 mm) and 11 sweep ⁵/₆₄-inch (2 mm)
- V-gouge: 45° / ³/₁₆-inch (5 mm)

PATTERN
Page 129

1 Transfer the pattern to the board.

2 Along the edges of the board mark the ¼-inch (6 mm) depth of the background to be removed (see page 33).

3 Go over the outline of the subject closely with a V-gouge and mallet.

4 Use a large 16 sweep ⁵/₈-inch (16 mm) gouge to lower the background to the marks (see page 34).

5 Cut in the design vertically; use the V-gouge in tight corners, and the 7 sweep ³/₈-inch (10 mm) medium gouge of the appropriate size on rounded surfaces.

6 Sculpt in the shapes using a 3 sweep ³/₈-inch (10 mm) shallow gouge, working from the highest part of the design. Mark off the outside shapes with a 5 sweep ½-inch (13 mm) shallow gouge or a 7 sweep ³/₈-inch (10 mm) medium gouge.

7 Smooth the bottoms inside the design with the small 3 sweep ³/₈-inch (10 mm) shallow gouge, or the 12 sweep ⁵/₁₆-inch (8 mm) cut in narrower areas.

8 Adjust the background using 21 ⁵/₁₆-inch (8 mm) and 3 ³/₈-inch (10 mm) sweeps. Always use the largest possible chisel because this creates the most appealing, clean surface. Don't forget the edges of the wood!

9 Finally, use a V-gouge and mallet to add decorative lines (see photo at right).

10 Glaze the design with the oil paint. Dilute the color with oil and apply sparingly. Let dry thoroughly (at least 24 hours), then carefully wipe off the excess with a paper towel.

11 For hanging, use a gouge to cut an oblong hole centered horizontally on the back.

FLOWERS IN RELIEF

Note

◆ Flower designs can also be mounted in an attractive picture frame (see sketch below).

Measurements

Picture: 4 x 6 inches (10.2 x 15.2 cm)

Frame: approximately 5½ x 7 inches (14 x 17.8 cm)

Cutout for picture: approximately 3½ x 5½ inches (8.9 x 14 cm)

Make the cutout for the picture with a coping saw. Note that the cutout must be approximately ¼ inch (6 mm) smaller than the glass all the way around. Use a V-gouge to cut in the groove on the back to accommodate the glass and the backing. Glazer's points for window frames (available from a hardware store or craft or photography shop) hold things together and make it possible to change pictures.

DEGREE OF DIFFICULTY

↺

SIZE

Flowers approximately 8 x 10¼ inches (20.3 x 26 cm)

MATERIALS

◆ 2 boxwood boards, each 8 x 11 inches (20.3 x 27.9 cm), a little over 1 inch (2.5 cm) thick
◆ Dark red, pink, green, and ochre oil paints
◆ Linseed oil
◆ Various small brushes

CARVING TOOLS

◆ Chisel: 2 sweep ³/₈-inch (10 mm)
◆ Shallow sweep gouges: 3 sweep ³/₁₆-inch (5 mm) and 3 sweep ⁵/₈-inch (16 mm)
◆ U-gouge: 10 sweep ¼-inch (6 mm)
◆ V-gouge: 45° / ³/₁₆-inch (5 mm)

PATTERNS

Pages 129 and 130

1 Using the pattern, transfer the design to the wood.

2 Mark the ¼-inch (6 mm) depth all around the edges of the wood (see page 33).

3 Use the V-gouge to go over the outlines of the design closely with the aid of the mallet.

4 Use the large 3 sweep ⁵/₈-inch (16 mm) shallow gouge to lower the background to the markings (see page 34).

5 Mark off the blocky design vertically with the 3 sweep ⁵/₈-inch (16 mm) shallow gouge. Sculpt the shape of the flower using the two shallow sweep gouges. The largest chisel should be used as much as possible to produce an appealing, even surface (see pages 34–35).

6 Clean up the lower parts with the 3 sweep ³/₁₆-inch (5 mm) shallow gouge and cut in the fine detail lines gracefully with the V-gouge. Use the 3 sweep ⁵/₈-inch (16 mm) shallow gouge to clean the saw marks from the edges of the wood.

7 Glaze the design with the appropriate colors as shown in the picture. Thin the paint with oil. Put some accents in ochre on the edges. Allow at least 24 hours for drying, then carefully wipe off excess oil with a paper towel.

8 For hanging, use a gouge to cut oblong holes centered horizontally on the backs.

CRUSHED CAN

Note

◆ The can pictured on page 69 is just one of countless possibilities; you can also use the two sketches on page 130 for starting points. You should carve the can at least double actual size or creating the bends and edges can be too difficult.

DEGREE OF DIFFICULTY
◔◔◔

SIZE
Approximately 12 inches (30.5 cm) tall

MATERIALS
◆ Section of dried chestnut log with bark removed, approx 10 inches (25.4 cm) in diameter and 12 inches (30.5 cm) tall
◆ Empty soft drink can
◆ Plaster
◆ White interior paint
◆ Flat paintbrush
◆ White or clear wax
◆ Soft cloth

CARVING TOOLS
◆ Shallow gouge: 3 sweep $^3/_{16}$-inch (5 mm) and 3 sweep $^5/_8$-inch (16 mm)
◆ Medium gouges: 7 sweep $^3/_8$-inch (10 mm) and 16 sweep $^5/_8$-inch (16 mm)
◆ U-gouges: 10 sweep $^1/_4$-inch (6 mm) and 11 sweep $^5/_{64}$-inch (2 mm)
◆ V-gouge: 45° / $^3/_{16}$-inch (5 mm)

1 Crush the empty can as desired. Mix up the plaster according to the directions, fill the can, and let it dry thoroughly so that the appearance of the can cannot change. Now paint the can with the interior paint.

2 Once the paint is dry, draw a centerline on the front and the side of the model. Several horizontal lines help to carry over the locations of the creases in the can, which is to be carved two to three times its actual size. Draw these lines carefully and completely from the start to the end of the individual creases.

3 Transfer the centerlines and horizontal lines to the section of wood. Keep redrawing these lines as wood is removed. Make sure that the distance between the horizontal lines is tripled.

4 Transfer all distinctive lines such as the rim of the can and the edges of all creases to the wood.

5 Set off the rim of the can with a V-gouge and lower the neck and the recessed top with the 16 sweep $^5/_8$-inch (16 mm) medium gouge, using the mallet as an aid.

6 Use the same medium gouge to sculpt the surfaces up to the crease.

7 Now cut the recesses under the creases with the 10 sweep $^1/_4$-inch (6 mm) U-gouge. Use the 11 sweep $^5/_{64}$-inch (2 mm) U-gouge in the tighter areas. Use the 16 sweep $^5/_8$-inch (16 mm) medium gouge to completely lay out the tapered recesses. Cut in the lower rim of the can with the 11 sweep $^5/_{64}$-inch (2 mm) gouge.

8 Smooth the upper surface with the 3 sweep $^5/_8$-inch (16 mm) shallow gouge. Use the 3 sweep $^3/_{16}$-inch (5 mm) in tighter areas.

9 Lay out the drinking hole with the V-gouge and clean it up with the small shallow gouge.

10 Finish the can with wax according to the manufacturer's instructions; after it's dry, polish it with a soft cloth.

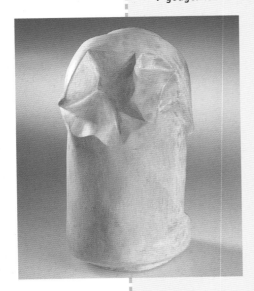

WEDDING DOVES BOX

Tips and Tricks

◆ To personalize the box further, you can carve in the name and the wedding date of the couple who will receive the gift.

◆ If the painting has to be done quickly, you can use dark-red acrylic paint instead of oil paint and linseed oil.

DEGREE OF DIFFICULTY

◔

SIZE

Dove figure approximately 2¹⁄₂ x 4³⁄₄ inches (6.4 x 12 cm)

MATERIALS

◆ A wooden box with a closure, approximately 4³⁄₄ x 8 x 4¹⁄₂ inches (12 x 20.3 x 11.4 cm)
◆ Small screwdriver
◆ Dark red oil paint
◆ Linseed oil
◆ Various small brushes
◆ Cream-colored fabric, 18 x 4¹⁄₂ inches (45.7 x 11.4 cm)
◆ White lace, 1 inch (2.5 cm) wide, approximately 20 inches (50.8 cm) long

CARVING TOOLS

◆ Shallow gouge: 3 sweep ³⁄₈-inch (10 mm)
◆ U-gouge: 11 sweep ⁵⁄₆₄-inch (2 mm)
◆ V-gouge: 45° / ³⁄₁₆-inch (5 mm)

PATTERN

Page 132

1 Use the screwdriver to remove the clasp from the box and take off the lid.

2 Paint a glaze of red paint on the top of the lid; dilute the oil paint with the linseed oil. Let everything dry thoroughly (24 hours). After drying, carefully remove excess oil with a paper towel.

3 Glue the fabric onto the box. First cut the sides to length and attach them with a very small amount of wood glue. Glue on the front part so that it overlaps approximately ³⁄₈ inch (1 cm).

4 Glue the lace to the top edge of the box and both vertical edges.

5 When this is dry, transfer the dove design to the wooden lid using tracing paper.

6 Incise the design with the V-gouge. Use a U-gouge to cut the larger curves of the wings and body, plus the smaller curves on the head, feathers, and heart. Use a shallow gouge to clean up all the lines in the tail feathers, plus the tapering, straight part.

7 Re-install the lid and the clasp.

WATER DIPPER BOWL

Tips and Tricks

◆ In order to achieve a uniform curvature on the inner and outer shapes of the bowl, templates in the shape of a quadrant are helpful; the curvature of the quarter-circle corresponds to the shape of the bowl. This way, as the work progresses the curvature can be checked regularly and adjusted as necessary.

◆ Here's a way to reduce the absorbency of the wood and to even out and solidify the surface a bit. Before scumbling, "paint" the entire surface of the bowl with thin liquid wood glue 2:1 with water.

DEGREE OF DIFFICULTY
◎◎◎

SIZE
Approximately 5¾ inches (14.6 cm) in diameter, 3 inches (7.6 cm) tall

MATERIAL
◆ Block of boxwood, approximately 6 x 6 x 3 inches (15.2 x 15.2 x 7.6 cm)
◆ Blue and white wood glazes
◆ Wood glue as needed
◆ Various small brushes
◆ Steel wool

CARVING TOOLS
◆ Shallow gouge: 3 sweep ⅝-inch (16 mm)
◆ Medium gouges: 7 sweep ⅜-inch (10 mm) and 16 sweep ⅝-inch (16 mm)
◆ U-gouge: 10 sweep ⅜-inch (10 mm)
◆ V-gouge: 45° / 3/16-inch (5 mm)

PATTERN
Page 132

1 Use the compass to lay out the inner and outer diameters of the bowl, plus the diameter of the base. In selecting or cutting out the block of wood, make sure that the fibers run vertically.

2 Clamp the block of wood securely. Start cutting in vertically with the shallow gouge along the circle for the outer diameter (using the mallet if necessary) to produce a cylindrical shape.

3 Now use the 10 sweep ⅜-inch (10 mm) U-gouge along the outline for the inner diameter. Change to a bent medium chisel with a 16 sweep ⅝-inch (16 mm) once a little depth is achieved. The goal is to produce a uniform hollow shape.

4 Draw a pencil line two-thirds of the way up the height of the bowl (outer cylinder shape) and use a shallow sweep to cut in all the way around at an angle of approximately 45°. Then remove wood from the upper edge of the bowl out to this cut. This procedure is repeated to produce a regular indentation of approximately ⅜ inch (1 cm) around the circumference.

5 First draw the contours of the edge, the indentation inside the bowl (in the shape of hands), and the wavy decoration on the rim of the bowl, and then carve them. Use a shallow gouge for shaping the edge and the 7 sweep ⅜-inch (10 mm) medium gouge for the wavy rim. After the contours inside the bowl (hands and fingers) are carved, open up the area between these cuts (the water) to approximately ⅛ inch (3 mm) with the 16 sweep ⅝ inch (16 mm) used previously.

6 Before removing the bowl from the clamp, rough out the outer curvature based on the wavy indentation (this is because of the curved edge and the thin rim the bowl cannot be clamped upside down). Now remove the bowl and use a shallow gouge to work the curvature evenly down to the line marked on the base of the bowl. In so doing, grasp the bowl firmly by hand, and if necessary brace it against the workbench or your thigh. Remember always to cut away from your body to avoid possible injury!

7 Paint the bowl as pictured, using blue and white glaze. Once the paint is dry, carefully rub the whole bowl with steel wool until the carving shows through the blue areas depicting water. Proceed in the same way with the white areas (the hands).

BAROQUE RELIEF

Notes

◆ Using a panel made of boards glued together can keep the wood from warping. A cabinetmaker can glue up boards for you.

Tips and Tricks

◆ Making a clay model assures proper spatial representation and helps in arranging the heights of the individual parts of the decoration.

◆ In executing the individual steps you should work circumferentially. Completing individual parts in detail is not helpful in achieving a unified overall picture.

◆ For a more intensive spatial composition, the outside edges can be undercut at certain places. This makes the volutes, scrollwork, and shell patterns appear even more three-dimensional.

DEGREE OF DIFFICULTY
◌◌◌

SIZE
Approximately 20 x 14½ inches (50.8 x 36.8 cm)

MATERIAL
◆ Boxwood board, 20 x 14½ inch (50.8 x 36.8 cm), approximately 1½ inch (3.8 cm) thick

CARVING TOOLS
◆ Chisels:
21 sweep ⁵/₁₆-inch (8 mm) and 2 sweep ³/₈-inch (10 mm)

◆ Shallow gouges:
3 sweep ³/₁₆-inch (5 mm), 3 sweep ⁵/₈-inch (16 mm), 4 sweep 1-inch (25 mm), 5 sweep ⁵/₁₆-inch (8 mm), and 5 sweep ¹¹/₁₆-inch (17 mm)

◆ Medium gouges:
7 sweep ³/₈-inch (10 mm) and 16 sweep ⁵/₈-inch (16 mm)

◆ Back bent medium gouge:
38 sweep ¼-inch (6 mm) (not part of basic equipment)

◆ U-gouges:
10 sweep ¼-inch (6 mm), 10 sweep ³/₈-inch (10 mm), and 11 sweep ⁵/₆₄-inch (2 mm)

PATTERNS
Pages 130 and 131

1 Transfer the design to the wood according to the pattern and clamp down securely. Lower the background marked on the panel to a depth of approximately ½ inch (1.3 cm) using the 10 sweep ¼-inch (6 mm) and 10 sweep ³/₈-inch (10 mm) U-gouges. For safety, stay approximately ³/₁₆ inch (5 mm) from the frame and the design.

2 Cut down vertically approximately ¾ inch (1.9 cm) to the background all along the outline of the design. Use a medium- or a shallow-sweep gouge as needed, depending on the outline. Place the gouge on the outline and drive it into the wood with one or two blows from the mallet. The gouges used are the 4 sweep 1-inch (25 mm), 5 sweep ⁵/₁₆-inch (8 mm), 5 sweep ¹¹/₁₆-inch (17 mm), 7 sweep ³/₈-inch (10 mm), and the 16 sweep ⁵/₈-inch (16 mm). To carve troublesome corners and crannies use a 2 sweep ³/₈-inch (10 mm) skew bevel chisel. For straight edges and smoothing the background cuts, use a 21 sweep ⁵/₁₆-inch (8 mm), 3 sweep ⁵/₈-inch (16 mm), and 4 sweep 1-inch (25 mm); a cut into the background deeper than the intended ¾ inch (1.9 cm) will require going over the entire background again.

3 Before carving the individual shapes of the relief design, the parts must be set apart from one another. Chisels used for the purpose are the 21 sweep ⁵/₁₆-inch (8 mm), 5 sweep ⁵/₁₆-inch (8 mm), 5 sweep ¹¹/₆₄-inch (4 mm), and 16 sweep ⁵/₈-inch (16 mm). The shell is lowered to approximately ³/₈ inch (1 cm) over the background at the level of the palmette and the volutes, rising slightly at the top edge. The palmette and the two adjoining volutes remain at their full height. The two outer volutes and the scrollwork taper down slightly to the outside. The cord projects approximately ³/₈ inch (1 cm) above the background. The following gouges are required: 3 sweep ⁵/₈-inch (16 mm), 4 sweep 1-inch (25 mm), 5 sweep ⁵/₈-inch (16 mm), and 16 sweep ⁵/₈-inch (16 mm). The back bent chisel (see the Note on page 100) is used to fashion the curves on the cord.

4 The surfaces of the two-dimensional elements at different heights are now given some stylistic treatment. The shell is decorated with transverse hollows using 7 sweep ³/₈-inch (10 mm) and 10 sweep ¼-inch (6 mm) gouges, and the palmette is given a fan structure with 3 sweep ⁵/₈-inch (16 mm) and 5 sweep ¹¹/₆₄-inch (4 mm) cuts. The outward curvature is applied to the volutes and the scrollwork. The cords are decorated with longitudinal grooves, as shown. The 11 sweep ⁵/₆₄-inch (2 mm) U-gouge is used for this. A note of caution: before adding these details, redraw the outlines of the individual parts onto the wood.

5 Finally, shape the frame. It consists of alternating series of even dips and notches that are carved with 16 sweep ⁵/₈-inch (16 mm) and 3 sweep ³/₁₆-inch (5 mm) cuts (or optionally with an appropriate V-gouge).

ORGANIC CANDLEHOLDERS

Tips and Tricks

◆ Since spruce is a soft wood, unappealing pressure dents can quickly result from the use of clamps, and the edge of the hole for the tea candle might be crushed. To prevent this, clamp the wood between small pieces of board.

DEGREE OF DIFFICULTY
👁👁

SIZE
Small candleholder, approximately 2¾ inches (7 cm)

Medium candleholder, approximately 4¼ inches (10.8 cm)

Large candleholder, approximately 6¼ inches (15.9 cm)

MATERIALS
◆ Blocks of spruce (not glued-up blocks); cross-section approximately 4¾ x 4¾ inches (12 x 12 cm), at least 13½ inches (34.3 cm) long

◆ 3 glass tea candle inserts

CARVING TOOLS
◆ Shallow gouges: 3 sweep ⅝-inch (16 mm) and 4 sweep 1-inch (25 mm)

◆ Medium gouges: 7 sweep ⅜-inch (10 mm) and 16 sweep ⅝-inch (16 mm)

OTHER TOOLS
◆ Handsaw

◆ Forstner drill bit, 1¾ inches (44 mm) diameter (the diameter depends on the size of the glass insert)

◆ Brass wire brush

◆ Propane torch

PATTERN
Page 133

1 Using the handsaw, cut the three blocks into lengths of 2¾ inches, 4¼ inches, and 6¼ inches (7 cm, 10.8 cm, and 15.9 cm).

2 Mark the center of the top of each block and drill a hole about ¾-inch (1.9 cm) deep with the 1¾-inch (44 mm) Forstner bit. Note: for drilling, the pieces of wood must be clamped securely.

3 Now carve the outer surfaces in succession. The resulting shape depends on each piece of wood, the number of knots, and perhaps the depth of the depressions. For carving, the wood must be clamped tightly in a vise or secured top and bottom between bench stops.

4 Work on the candleholders side by side with the appropriate chisels. Shape any existing depressions into a V using the 3 sweep ⅝-inch (16 mm) shallow gouge. The knots are freed up with a medium gouge, and trough-shaped depressions are carved into the surfaces. The corners and the transitions to the bottom and top sides are carved with both gouges. The final form for the candleholders is up to you. Sanding is not necessary.

5 The completely carved candleholders are then treated as described in the "Burning" paragraph in the chapter on surface treatment (page 56).

CLASSICAL FIGURES

Tips and Tricks

◆ If you want to carve designs of your own creation, first model them in clay (available in hobby and pottery supply shops) and let them dry thoroughly. Then transfer the contours from the model to the wood using a grid pattern. This makes it easy even for beginning carvers to create sculptural reliefs.

DEGREE OF DIFFICULTY
◔◔◔

SIZE
Approximately 15¾ inches (40 cm) tall

MATERIAL FOR EACH WALL HANGING
◆ Maple board 15¾ x 9 inches (40 x 22.9 cm), a little over 1 inch (2.5 cm) thick

CARVING TOOLS
◆ Shallow gouges: 3 sweep ³/₁₆-inch (5 mm), 3 sweep ⁵/₈-inch (16 mm), and 5 sweep ⁵/₁₆-inch (8 mm)
◆ Medium gouge: 7 sweep ³/₈-inch (10 mm)
◆ U-gouge: 11 sweep ⁵/₆₄-inch (2 mm)
◆ V-gouge: 45° / ³/₁₆-inch (5 mm)

PATTERNS
Pages 127 and 129

1   Transfer the pattern to the wood.

2   Saw the wood into the appropriate shape.

3   Set in the outlines of the highest areas of the design (rocks, cloth, head, and heels) with the V-gouge.

4   Rough out the body and the clouds with the 5 sweep ⁵/₁₆-inch (8 mm) shallow gouge to a depth of approximately ¼ inch (6 mm). Go over the outline of the clouds with the V-gouge and lower the background of the design by another ³/₁₆ inch (5 mm); see page 34.

5   Rough out the sculptural curves of the rocky structure with the 5 sweep ⁵/₁₆-inch (8 mm) medium gouge and cut the folds in the cloth with the U-gouge. Use the V-gouge to create the sharp edges on the cloth and the rocks. Clean up the coarse surface of the rocks with fine cuts with the 3 sweep ⁵/₈-inch (16 mm) shallow gouge. Shape the folds in the cloth with the 3 sweep ³/₁₆-inch (5 mm) shallow gouge and smooth the surface. Take care to remove very little wood as you smooth.

6   Now sculpt the preliminary shape of the body and the sky using the 5 sweep ⁵/₁₆-inch (8 mm) shallow gouge; use the 7 sweep ³/₈-inch (10 mm) medium gouge on the recesses and the U-gouge for the deep lines. As soon as the major shapes are visible, smooth and clean them up with the 3 sweep ⁵/₈-inch (16 mm) shallow gouge and the 3 sweep ³/₁₆-inch (5 mm) in the narrower places. Set the shapes off from the background with the V-gouge.

7   Carve the background cleanly using a guided cut.

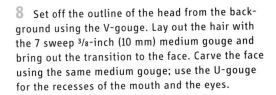

8   Set off the outline of the head from the background using the V-gouge. Lay out the hair with the 7 sweep ³/₈-inch (10 mm) medium gouge and bring out the transition to the face. Carve the face using the same medium gouge; use the U-gouge for the recesses of the mouth and the eyes.

9   Carve the shapes of the laid-out head and face smoothly and cleanly using very small, careful cuts with the 3 sweep ³/₁₆-inch (5 mm) shallow gouge. Add vibrant lines to the hair with the U-gouge.

10   Use the 3 sweep ⁵/₈-inch (16 mm) shallow gouge to clean up the rim of the wood to the sawed edges all the way around.

11   For hanging, carve a horizontal, oblong hole centered in the back.

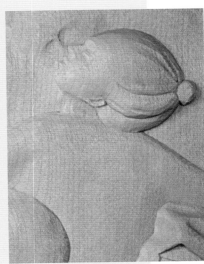

DECORATIONS
FOR OUTDOORS

HOUSE NUMBER & DOOR SIGN

House Number

1 Transfer the design to the wood from the pattern.

2 Lower the surface between the frame and the numbers using both U-gouges to a depth of approximately 1 inch (2.5 cm). Cut in the inner wall vertically down to the background (see pages 34 and 36).

3 Clean up the corners and smooth the surface with the shallow sweep gouge.

4 Stipple the background as described on page 57. This produces a surface that appears uniform even in the background areas that are difficult to reach. Fairly small irregularities in the carving can likewise be disguised.

5 Waterproof the sign if desired using clear varnish. The background can also be stained a little darker to create a clearer contrast.

6 If desired, attach a hanger on the backside, or drill a pair of holes in the relief and anchor it with dowels.

Door Sign

1 Transfer the design to the wood from the pattern; cut out along the outline and clamp the wood securely.

2 Lower the surface of the house wall for the name and the fence using the 11 sweep 5/64-inch (2 mm) gouge to a depth of approximately 5/64-inch (2 mm); see page 34.

3 Likewise use the gouge to lower the roof, from the gutter to the ridgeline, to an even depth of approximately 3/16-inch (5 mm). In so doing, the cat, the chimney, and the inscription "Family" stand out in relief and the outline of the tree becomes visible.

4 Use the gouge to structure the surface of the tree as pictured, or any other way you wish, and cut in around the bird at a distance of approximately 1/32 inch (1 mm). Sand the piece lightly.

5 Stipple evenly on the wall of the house and the roof, as well as the area around the bird. Now the individual designs stand out in sharp relief (see page 57).

6 Color the design with watercolors as pictured and cover the surface with waterproof varnish.

DEGREE OF DIFFICULTY
◔◔

SIZE
House number approximately 7 x 5 inches (17.5 cm x 13 cm)

Door sign 7½ x 11 inches (19 cm x 27 cm)

MATERIALS FOR HOUSE NUMBER
- Oak board approximately 7 x 5 inches (17.5 x 13 cm)
- Stippling punch

DOOR SIGN
- Oak board approximately 8 by 12 inches (20 x 30 cm), a little more than 1 inch (3 cm) thick
- Red, brown, green, yellow, and black watercolors
- Opaque white primer
- Various small brushes
- Stippling punch

CARVING TOOLS FOR HOUSE NUMBER
- Shallow gouge: 3 sweep 3/16-inch (5 mm)
- U-gouges: 10 sweep 1/4-inch (6 mm) and 11 sweep 5/64-inch (5/2)

DOOR SIGN
- U-gouge: 11 sweep 5/64-inch (2 mm)

PATTERN
Pages 133 and 134

Tips and Tricks

◆ The door sign and the house number should be made of hardwood if placed outside in the elements. If they are sheltered by something like a porch, a soft wood can be used.

◆ The wood around the numbers can also be removed with a router, and a drill press with a depth stop helps rough out the design.

◆ In creating the house number you can create an interesting contrast between the light wood and a dark background that makes the numbers easier to read from a distance.

◆ Bevel the edges to avoid creating pockets where water can collect.

WISE OLD OWL

Tips and Tricks

◆ Pierce the cavity at the sides of the owl through to the rear of the trunk. That way the owl can also be carved from the rear, and the effect is more realistic.

◆ If the carving is to be kept outdoors, make sure it has no surfaces where water can collect by beveling the edges.

◆ Bark that is splitting off should first be secured with liquid glue and a small, nearly invisible brad.

◆ Place the owl in a place sheltered from the weather and intense sunlight. If the owl suffers minor damage, you can go over the carving again and paint over the repair, but before you apply paint, the wood must be completely dry.

DEGREE OF DIFFICULTY
◔◔◔

SIZE
Approximately 30 inches (76.2 cm) tall

MATERIALS
◆ Section of boxwood trunk, approximately 12 inches (30.5 cm) in diameter and 28 inches (71.1 cm) tall and 6 inches (15.2 cm) thick
◆ Light green, dark green, brown, orange, and black watercolors
◆ Black felt tip pen

CARVING TOOLS
◆ Shallow gouges:
3 sweep ³/₈-inch (10 mm) and 3 sweep ⁵/₈-inch (16 mm)
◆ Medium gouges:
7 sweep ³/₈-inch (10 mm) and 16 sweep ⁵/₈-inch (16 mm)
◆ U-gouges:
10 sweep ¹/₄-inch (6 mm),
10 sweep ³/₈-inch (10 mm),
and 11 sweep ⁵/₆₄-inch (2 mm)
◆ V-gouge: 45° / ³/₁₆-inch (5 mm)

PATTERN
Page 134

1 Transfer the design to the section of tree trunk with a template or tracing paper and darken the lines with a felt tip pen.

2 Cut into the bark inside the marked-off area with a shallow sweep gouge and carve away the bark until the light-colored wood becomes visible.

3 Draw the owl, complete with head, wings, and feet, on the light surface of the wood. Use a shallow sweep gouge to cut in for a distance of a little over 1 inch (2.5 cm) and to a depth of 1½ inches (3.8 cm), so that the front of the owl is visible in outline form.

4 Shape the head, belly, wings, and feet with the shallow gouges, medium gouges, and U-gouges. The V-gouge is useful in making dividing lines, as between the body and the wings. The surfaces must continually be rounded to give the body a harmonious overall appearance (see pages 36–37).

5 Carve the feathers with the medium sweep gouge, and the claws with the V-gouge. For the breast feathers, cut in vertically with the curved medium gouge, as with the radius stop cut, and cut into it from below at an angle of approximately 30°. This removes an oblique chip and produces the impression of raised feathers.

6 Paint the protruding parts of the plumage in light and dark green, and the beak in brown. Make the eyes and claws orange, and the pupils black. Paint the recesses around the subject a little darker to set if off visually from the tree. Waterproof the owl and all the recesses with matte varnish.

SNAIL

Tips and Tricks

◆ Under the feelers on the head you can also carve a simple face or paint it before you varnish the figure.

◆ The snail turns into a comical and colorful eye-catcher when children paint the shell in many colors.

DEGREE OF DIFFICULTY
◔◔

SIZE
Approximately 10 inches (25.4 cm) long, 5½ inches (14 cm) tall

MATERIAL
◆ Block of boxwood, 10 x 5½ x 4 inches (25.4 x 14 x 10.2 cm)

CARVING TOOLS
◆ Shallow gouge:
3 sweep ³⁄₈-inch (10 mm)

◆ Medium gouge:
7 sweep ³⁄₈-inch (10 mm)

◆ U-gouge: 10 sweep ¼-inch (6 mm),
10 sweep ³⁄₈-inch (10 mm),
and 11 sweep ⁵⁄₆₄-inch (2 mm)

PATTERN
Page 135

1 Transfer the outline of the figure to the wood and saw off the unneeded parts of wood, or carve them off square to the outside surface using the gouges. Use a clamp to hold the block down or screw the flattened piece of wood to a base plate that sticks out at least 2 inches (5.1 cm), securing it with clamps.

2 Shape all around the body of the snail (without the shell) using the medium gouge and the U-gouges. Round the shell evenly on all sides. Then use the pattern to draw the spiral for the shell, as shown, and shape it with the gouges (see pages 43–44).

3 Now add the details to the surface of the figure. Carefully smooth the shell with the shallow gouge. If necessary, sand the shell and add some contrast to the body with grooves, using the medium gouge .

4 If the snail is to be placed in the yard, coat it with clear varnish and let it dry thoroughly (see page 55).

THE GREEN MAN

Tips and Tricks

◆ Stand or hang this sculpture under cover to keep it protected from wind and weather.

◆ Reattach loose bark with wood glue. Let the glue set, and attach the bark with some additional nails, first countersinking the heads of the nails halfway into the bark. Then glue a piece of bark over the repair.

DEGREE OF DIFFICULTY
◔◔◔

SIZE
Approximately 20 inches (50.8 cm)

MATERIALS
◆ Piece of boxwood log approximately 12 inches (30.5 cm) in diameter, 20 inches (50.8 cm) tall, and 4 inches (10.2 cm) thick

◆ Watercolors or acrylic paints in white, brown, black, and pink

CARVING TOOLS
◆ Bent chisel: 21 sweep $^5/_{16}$-inch (8 mm)

◆ Shallow gouges: 3 sweep $^3/_8$-inch (10 mm) and 3 sweep $^5/_8$-inch (16 mm)

◆ Medium gouge: 7 sweep $^3/_8$-inch (10 mm)

◆ U-gouges: 10 sweep $^3/_8$-inch (10 mm) and 11 sweep $^5/_{64}$-inch (2 mm)

◆ V-gouge: 45° / $^3/_{16}$-inch (5 mm)

PATTERN
Page 135

1 Transfer the face design to the section of log as described on page 82; use a shallow gouge to cut into the bark and remove it in the face area. The eyebrows should be left in place, or they can be cut from the removed pieces of bark and glued and nailed back in place after the face is done.

2 Cut out the recesses for the eyes (surface 1; see sketch below) inside the drawn outline to a depth of a little over 1 inch (2.5 cm) with gouges and half-round chisels. Level the bottom with the bent chisel.

3 Use the U-gouges and the V-gouge to lower the mouth and chin (surface 2; see sketch below)

beneath the tip of the nose and inside the cheeks to a depth of approximately 1½ inches (3.8 c▮

4 Cut in for the inside of mout▮ (surface 3; see sketch below) w▮ the same gouges to a depth of a little more than 1 inch (2.5 cm) and shape the slightly rounded tongue and upper row of teeth.

5 Uniformly lower and round ▮ nose from the highest point at t▮ tip back to the bridge. A thick p▮ nose looks particularly neat.

6 Paint the eyes to look lifelik▮ with watercolor or acrylic paint▮ necessary, adjust them so that both eyes look in the same dire▮ tion. Paint the row of teeth whi▮ and the tongue and lower lip w▮ pink highly diluted with water.

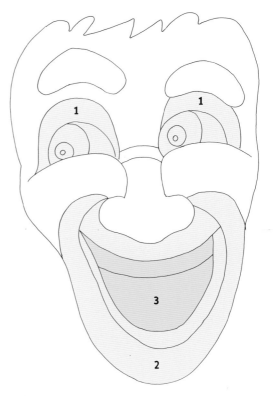

RUSTIC ROOSTERS

1 Body: Use a hand saw to cut the section of branch for the tail into strips from 5/64 to 1/8 inch (2 to 3 mm) thick; carefully bend these strips downward and keep them tied in place with string or wire (see photo below) for two days. This is quite easy to do with fresh-cut wood. You can also use older wood if you place the sawn strips in water for a day and then bend them in shape.

2 Fashion two pointed legs on the lower end with a shallow sweep gouge and flatten the head part on both sides.

3 Use the hand saw to cut out the contour of the head and create the final shape with the shallow gouge and U-gouge. Shape the throat as you wish and use the V-gouge to carve in some lines that suggest plumage.

4 Measure the distance between the feet and drill holes in the second forked stick as a base for the figure.

5 Attach the rooster to the forked stick by the legs, as shown; if necessary, use a little wood glue.

6 Paint the comb and the wattle red; use a dot of black permanent marker for each eye.

DEGREE OF DIFFICULTY

SIZE
Approximately 8 to 12 inches
(20.3 to 30.5 cm)

**MATERIALS
FOR EACH ROOSTER**
- 2 forked birch branches (for body and base), approximately 12 to 14 inches (30.5 to 35.6 cm) long
- Red acrylic paint
- Small brush
- Black permanent marker
- Drill bits of various sizes (depending on the diameters of the feet)
- Hand saw

CARVING TOOLS
- Shallow gouge:
  5 sweep 1/2-inch (13 mm)
- Medium gouge:
  7 sweep 3/8-inch (10 mm)
- U-gouge: 11 sweep 5/64-inch (2 mm)
- V-gouge: 45° / 3/16-inch (5 mm)

PATTERN
Page 136

Tips and Tricks

◆ If you can't find any appropriate branches for a curved rooster tail, you can easily make one by sawing a fresh branch (such as of birch or hazel) into five to eight strips approximately 5/64 inch (2 mm) thick. Tie the strips together, bend them into a U shape, secure them with clamps, and let them dry for two days. Glue the strips as pictured so that they are separated by a space; fashion a point on one end and glue it into a hole.

EASTER BUNNY

Tips and Tricks

◆ A rasp and sandpaper make it easier to round areas where the grain has a lot of curl.

DEGREE OF DIFFICULTY
◎◎

SIZE
Approximately 22 inches
(55.9 cm) tall

MATERIALS
◆ A section of boxwood log approximately 4 inches (10.2 cm) in diameter, 22 inches (55.9 cm) long
◆ Watercolor or acrylic paint in nougat, white, and black

CARVING TOOLS
◆ Shallow gouge:
5 sweep ½-inch (13 mm)
◆ Medium gouge:
7 sweep ⅜-inch (10 mm)
◆ U-gouges: 10 sweep ¼-inch (6 mm), 10 sweep ⅜-inch (10 mm), and 11 sweep 5/64-inch (2 mm)

PATTERN
Page 136

1 Transfer the design to the section of log. Carve out the area between the ears with the half-round chisel or saw it out.

2 First round the ears slightly on the outsides and then the insides, and hollow them out according to the pattern and the illustration.

3 Carve the head with the U-gouges and the shallow sweep gouge; keep turning the wood as you work to produce even contours and proportions. Draw on the eyes and then shape them using a small U-gouge.

4 Shape the torso, paws, and hind legs to scale using the U-gouges.

5 Color the muzzle, paws, and hind legs in nougat; prime the eyes in white, and paint on black pupils with a white spot of reflected light.

AFRICAN MASKS

Tips and Tricks

◆ Long, unpainted masks are also attractive. Choose a wood with a plain, unpretentious grain so that the face shows to full advantage.

DEGREE OF DIFFICULTY
◯◯

HEIGHT
Painted mask approximately 14 inches (35.6 cm) tall

Unpainted mask approximately 15¾ inches (40 cm) tall

MATERIALS
◆ Boxwood log, 9 x 14 inches (22.9 x 35.6 cm), 2 inches (5.1 cm) thick (painted mask)

◆ Boxwood log, 4¾ x 15¾ inches (12 x 40 cm), 2 inches (5.1 cm) thick (unpainted mask)

◆ Dark brown and teak wood stain

◆ Gilding adhesive and a small brush

  ◆ Gold leaf (1 sheet)

  ◆ Soft, clean small brush

  ◆ Soft cloth

CARVING TOOLS
◆ Shallow gouge: 3 sweep ⅝-inch (16 mm)

◆ Medium gouges: 7 sweep ⅜-inch (10 mm) and 16 sweep ⅝-inch (16 mm)

◆ V-gouge: 45° / 3/16-inch (5 mm)

PATTERNS
Pages 136 and 137

1 Transfer the design to the piece of wood using the patte and cut along the outline with the jigsaw. In so doing, it's helpful to cut in from the outside to the edge of the subject every 2 inches (5.1 cm). That way the individual segments fa off and the saw blade does not bind.

2 Use the V-gouge to cut around the nose and mouth and the 16 sweep ⅝-inch (16 mm) medium gouge to lower the a around the face (except for the forehead) to a depth of approximately ¾ inch (1.9 cm) and cut and taper the side edges toward the back. This will keep the wood from splitti

3 Use the 16 sweep ⅝-inch (16 mm) medium gouge to shape th decoration on the head and neck, and smooth it with the 3 swee ⅝-inch (16 mm). Cut around the circular shapes vertically w the 16 sweep ⅝-inch (16 mm) medium gouge and carve the arch circular area with the 7 sweep ⅜-inch (10 mm) medium gouge. Sculpt the feathered ornament on the unpainted ma with the 7 sweep ⅜-inch (10 mm) medium gouge. Lines applied sparingly with the V-gouge give the design a life-li appearance.

4 Starting at the tip of the nose, slightly lower the forehea lips, and wings of the nose and taper the side edges of the face. Use small cuts with the small 7 sweep ⅜-inch (10 mm) medium gouge downward from the tip of the nose to produc the shapes of the nose and the transition to the eyes, cheek mouth, and chin. Accentuate the sharp edges at the eyes, li and nose with the V-gouge.

5 Go over the eyelids with the V-gouge and set off the eyeba with a 7 sweep ⅜-inch (10 mm) medium gouge. Use a rotati motion with the gouge to cut in the pupils (see page 26).

6 Before cutting in the fine lines, lightly stain the head, chin, and earrings with the dark brown stain (follow the ma ufacturer's directions). Allow it to dry thoroughly. Treat the remaining surfaces with the teak stain. As soon as the stain dry, apply the fine lines with the V-gouge. (The mallet is he ful for this.)

7 Apply the gilding adhesive sparingly to the surfaces to b gilded and let it set for five minutes. Now place onto those areas piece of gold leaf cut to size, carefully brushing and attachi each with the brush. After the gold leaf has dried for about minutes, excess can be removed by rubbing it with the cloth

8 For hanging on a wall, use a drill to make an oblong, ho zontal hole centered on the back.

SUN

Tips and Tricks

◆ Once you have had some carving practice you can also carve the eyes and the mouth to make them stand out more dramatically.

DEGREE OF DIFFICULTY
◐◐

SIZE
Approximately 10 inches (25.4 cm) in diameter

MATERIAL
◆ Pine board, approximately 10 x 10 inches (25.4 x 25.4 cm), a little over 1 inch (2.5 cm) thick

CARVING TOOLS
◆ Shallow gouge: 3 sweep $^3/_8$-inch (10 mm)
◆ Medium gouge: 7 sweep $^3/_8$-inch (10 mm)
◆ U-gouges: 10 sweep $^1/_4$-inch (6 mm) and 11 sweep $^5/_{64}$-inch (2 mm)
◆ V-gouge: 45° / $^3/_{16}$-inch (5 mm)
◆ Watercolors in yellow, blue, red, and black
◆ Black fine-tip permanent marker

PATTERN
Page 138

1 Transfer the design to the wood, saw it out, and clamp it down.

2 Draw the round face of the sun (not counting the rays, approximately 5 inches [12.7 cm] in diameter). Use the gouges to make a groove around the circle approximately $^3/_8$ inch (1 cm) deep.

3 Arch the outlined face portion evenly from the center and outward toward the groove using the shallow gouge (see page 34). Use the medium gouge to suggest slight recesses for the eyes, mouth, and the cheek areas next to the nose. Use sandpaper to create harmonious, smooth transitions to the recesses.

4 Use the medium gouge to arch the crown of rays inward toward the groove, and taper them outward to flame-like points (see page 35).

5 Draw the individual rays again, set them off with the U-gouges and the V-gouge, and work them to different heights. Flatten the rays toward the ends. Some irregular indentations using the V-gouge give the rays verve and liveliness (see page 35).

6 Prime the sun in yellow. Apply plenty of orange highly thinned with water to the still moist, raised parts of the face and rays, and immediately wipe them with the cloth to produce watercolor-type transitions. Daub some watery blue into the still-damp groove around the face to produce subtle greenish-blue transitions. Carefully mix the colors using only a little water so they don't run.

7 After the sun is dry, draw on the shapes of the eyes and the mouth with the permanent marker and color them in. Finally, waterproof the design with a matte varnish.

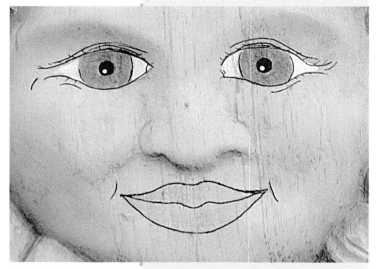

FRUIT

Tips and Tricks

◆ You'll find lots of ideas in the supermarket! For an interesting challenge, try a partly peeled banana, a piece of melon, or a pineapple. Before you start, try to have a detailed illustration or photo of each subject.

DEGREE OF DIFFICULTY

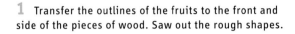

SIZE FOR PIECES SHOWN

Apple approximately 3½ inches (8.9 cm) tall

Pear approximately 3½ inches (8.9 cm) tall

Banana approximately 8 inches (20.3 cm) long

MATERIALS

◆ Block of boxwood, 3½ x 3½ x 3½ inches (8.9 x 8.9 x 8.9 cm) for an apple; 2½ x 2½ x 3½ inches (6.4 x 6.4 x 8.9 cm) for a pear; and 8 x 2½ x 2 inches (20.3 x 6.4 x 5.1 cm) for a banana

CARVING TOOLS

◆ Shallow gouge:
3 sweep ⅝-inch (16 mm)

◆ Medium gouges:
7 sweep ⅜-inch (10 mm) and 16 sweep ⅝-inch (16 mm)

1   Transfer the outlines of the fruits to the front and side of the pieces of wood. Saw out the rough shapes.

2   Roughly shape the contours with the 16 sweep ⅝-inch (16 mm) curved medium gouge.

3   Rough-cut the area for the stem and the blossom with the 7 sweep ⅜-inch (10 mm) medium gouge. Lay out the stems nearly 1 inch long and 1 inch thick (2.5 x 2.5 cm), making sure that the stems are kept thick for as long as possible so they don't break off during the work.

4   Level the surface with the 3 sweep ⅝-inch (16 mm) shallow gouge and work the stem down to an appropriate size.

5   Cut in the area for the stem with the 7 sweep ⅜-inch (10 mm) medium gouge so that it looks natural. The underside should be flat in the center; use the 3 sweep ⅝-inch (16 mm) shallow gouge to make several chip cuts in different directions.

6   Smooth the edges of the surface cuts with coarse sandpaper.

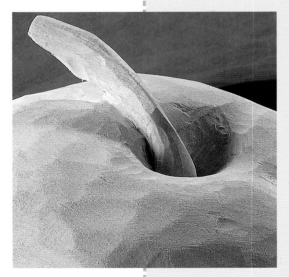

COLORFUL FISH

Tips and Tricks

◆ A rasp can be used for roughing out shapes.

◆ For a simpler version, cut in around the eyes and paint the insides.

◆ Mount the fishes on stands by carefully drilling a hole into the narrow underside of the body (belly or fins) and inserting a metal rod secured in an overturned clay saucer.

DEGREE OF DIFFICULTY

SIZE

Blue and yellow fish: approximately 7 inches (17.8 cm) long

Red fish: approximately 5 inches (12.7 cm) tall

Orange-red fish approximately 4 inches (10.2 cm) tall

MATERIALS FOR 3 FISHES

◆ Boxwood, Eastern white pine, or Swiss stone pine board, approximately 9 x 12 inches (22.9 x 30.5 cm), a little over 1 inch (2.5 cm) thick

◆ Scrap wood approximately 3/16 inch (5 mm) thick, for fins

◆ Red, orange, yellow, blue, and black watercolors

◆ White primer

◆ Scrap cardboard

◆ 3 thumbtacks with red or white plastic heads

◆ Black permanent marker

CARVING TOOLS

◆ Medium gouge: 7 sweep 3/8-inch (10 mm)

◆ U-gouges: 10 sweep 1/4-inch (6 mm) and 11 sweep 5/64-inch (2 mm)

PATTERNS

Pages 138 and 139

1 Transfer each fish design to the selected wood and saw it out.

2 Place the rough shape of a fish flat on the work surface and clamp it in the center of the body (the thickest part). Place a piece of cardboard between the clamp and the fish to prevent denting in the wood.

3 Shape the body with the medium gouge so that it tapers at the head and the ends of the fins and flattens on all sides to produce a streamlined shape. The center of the body should be the thickest and most compact area of the fish.

4 Carve the individual fins for the blue-yellow and orange-red fish separately, by hand, and according to the pattern. Decorate the fins with incised lines, using the 11 sweep 5/64-inch (2 mm) gouge .

5 Make the hollows for the eyes with the gouges.

6 Remove the fish from the clamp for final shaping. Place the fish on the underlay, hold it firmly, and round and smooth the previously untreated surfaces first with coarse and then fine sandpaper.

7 Paint the fishes and fins as pictured. To achieve the richest coloration, use several coats of paint. Let each coat dry before repainting and sand off any raised fibers of wood with fine sandpaper. Varying the pressure on the sandpaper will produce interesting lighter and darker colors. Push a white or red thumbtack into the eye socket and color the pupil with black permanent marker (see photo).

8 Attach the fins on top and bottom with wood glue. It's best to follow the photos and the pattern. A coat of gloss varnish gives the fish a natural wet appearance.

A RELIEF-CARVED HEAD OF GRAIN

Notes

◆ With this design (as with the Baroque Relief project on page 75) it's necessary to use a back-bent chisel to create curvatures that are difficult to achieve with a straight chisel.

◆ A skew chisel is also effective for working with difficult-to-reach areas.

◆ After unclamping the completed relief you can create a frame around the background approximately 1 inch (2.5 cm) wide and 3/8 inch (1 cm) high with a 1 sweep 1½-inch (38 mm) chisel (not part of the basic equipment); this gives the relief a more elegant appearance and greater apparent distance from the wall.

DEGREE OF DIFFICULTY

◔◔

SIZE

Approximately 9½ inches (24.1 cm) tall

MATERIALS FOR EACH RELIEF

◆ Boxwood board, approximately 9½ x 4¾ inches (24.1 x 12 cm), 9/16 inch (1.4 cm) thick

◆ Liquid glue

◆ White, blue, green, brown, yellow, and orange oil paints

◆ Various small brushes

CARVING TOOLS

◆ Chisel: 2 sweep 3/8 inch (10 mm)

◆ Shallow gouges: 3 sweep 3/16-inch (5 mm), 5 sweep 5/16-inch (8 mm), and 5 sweep 11/16-inch (17 mm)

◆ Medium gouge: 7 sweep 3/8-inch (10 mm)

◆ Back-bent half-round chisels: 38 sweep 5/32-inch (3 mm) and 38 sweep 3/8-inch (10 mm) (not part of the basic equipment)

◆ U-gouges: 10 sweep 1/4-inch (6 mm) and 11 sweep 5/64-inch (2 mm)

◆ V-gouge: 45° / 3/16-inch (5 mm)

PATTERN

Page 140

1 Transfer the design to the board and clamp the wood down firmly for working.

2 Lower the areas between the stalks, leaves, and grain heads (the background) to a depth of about a little more than 1/4 inch (6 mm). If desired, mark the depth all around the sides of the board. Use the 10 sweep 1/4-inch (6 mm) gouge to make a groove approximately 5/64 inch (2 mm) from the outlines and lower the surfaces. Then level the surfaces with the 5 sweep 5/16-inch (8 mm) and 5 sweep 11/16-inch (17 mm) shallow gouges (see also page 34).

3 Now cut straight down to the background around the outlines of the design using the appropriate carving tools, using the mallet if necessary. Remove the cut wood with a shallow gouge and a chisel and gradually create the desired background depth (see page 34).

4 Once all the parts of the design are freed up, you can begin with the detailed shaping. Lower the awns (bristles) from the seeds toward the outside with the 3 sweep 3/16-inch (5 mm) shallow gouge to a height of approximately 5/64-inch (2 mm) above the background. Carve the stalks and the leaves with the back-bent medium gouge. The 7 sweep 3/16-inch (5 mm) and 11 sweep 5/64-inch (2 mm) gouges and the V-gouge are used for shaping the seeds and the individual awns.

5 Now the frame of the relief is carved in the shape of a quarter-round with the 38 sweep 3/8-inch (10 mm) chisel. First cut a dividing line in the bevels to keep the wood from splitting at the edges.

6 Paint the relief as desired. The design on the left was painted with oils as follows: First the relief was painted with sizing by mixing liquid glue and water in a 2:1 proportion and using a small brush to coat the entire surface. After drying thoroughly, it was painted as pictured with oil paints. After the relief dried thoroughly again, a clear varnish (or hairspray) is applied as a fixative.

TREES

Tips and Tricks

◆ The outer edges of the trees can be carved with a hand-held carving knife. Caution: it's better for beginners to clamp the piece down to reduce the chance of injury.

DEGREE OF DIFFICULTY

↻

SIZE

Left tree: approximately
8¾ x 8 inches (22.2 x 20.3 cm)

Middle tree: approximately
7 x 5¾ inches (17.8 x 14.6 cm)

Right tree: approximately
11 x 4¾ inches (27.9 x 12 cm)

MATERIALS

◆ Boxwood board 1 inch (2.5 cm) thick
Left tree approximately
8¾ x 8 inches (22.2 x 20.3 cm)

Middle tree: approximately
7 x 6 inches (17.8 x 15.2 cm)

Right tree: approximately
11 x 4¾ inches (27.9 x 12 cm)

All together approximately
12 x 18 inches (30.5 x 45.7 cm)

CARVING TOOLS

◆ Shallow gouges:
3 sweep ⅜-inch (10 mm),
3 sweep ⅝-inch (16 mm),
and 5 sweep ½-inch (13 mm)

◆ U-gouge: 10 sweep ¼-inch (6 mm)

◆ Carving knife

◆ V-gouge: 45° / 3/16-inch (5 mm)
and ⅜-inch (10 mm)

PATTERN
Page 141

1 Transfer the trees to the board according to the pattern, saw them out, and clamp them down.

2 Use the V-gouge to cut along the drawn lines and the shallow gouges to create the varying heights either as pictured or according to your own sense of shape. Recess the lower areas to a depth of approximately 3/16 to ⅜ inch (5 to 10 mm) so that the foliage stands out in relief.

3 Cut the branches and the leaves slightly deeper with the V-gouges.

4 Use the 3 sweep ⅜-inch (10 mm) shallow gouge on the sharp edges, and then clean up the surfaces.

5 Use the gouge to give the foliage a cloudlike shape and clean up the whole design. At the end the branches and the trunk should be lower than the foremost foliage.

6 Finally, clean up the outer edges with the 3 sweep ⅜-inch (10 mm) shallow gouge.

ADVENT WREATH & TEA LIGHT HOLDER

Tips and Tricks

◆ You can make the candle and tea light holders quickly and easily by using a Forstner bit in an electric drill and a drill stand. Caution: lower the bit slowly into the wood so that the edge does not split.

◆ In order to protect the advent wreath from dripped wax and dirt, coat the whole surface with clear varnish.

◆ To get rid of dripped wax, use a hair drier to melt the wax, then wipe it off with a rag.

◆ Beeswax candles not only look good in this advent wreath, but excess wax can be rubbed in to give the unvarnished wood a decorative and protective coating.

DEGREE OF DIFFICULTY

◔◔

SIZE

Advent wreath, approximately 10 inches (25.4 cm) in diameter

Table light approximately 6¼ inches (15.9 cm) tall, approximately 4 inches (10.2 cm) wide and 4¾ inches (12 cm) deep

MATERIALS ADVENT WREATH

◆ Eastern white or Swiss stone pine log, approximately 10 inches (25.4 cm) long, 2 inches (5.1 cm) thick

◆ Stippling punch or nail

◆ 4 candles, approximately 1 inch (2.5 cm) in diameter

CARVING TOOLS

◆ Medium gouge: 16 sweep ⅝-inch (16 mm)

◆ U-gouges: 10 sweep ¼-inch (6 mm) and 11 sweep ⁵⁄₆₄-inch (2 mm)

◆ V-gouge: 45° / ³⁄₁₆-inch (5 mm)

MATERIALS TEA LIGHT HOLDER

◆ Block of boxwood, approximately 6¼ x 4 x 4 ¾ inches (15.9 x 10.2 x 12 cm)

◆ Tea light with glass cup

CARVING TOOLS

◆ Shallow gouge: 3 sweep ³⁄₁₆-inch (5 mm)

◆ Medium gouges: 7 sweep ⅜-inch (10 mm) and 16 sweep ⅝-inch (16 mm)

◆ U-gouges: 10 sweep ¼-inch (6 mm), 10 sweep ⅜-inch (10 mm), and 11 sweep ⁵⁄₆₄-inch (2 mm)

◆ V-gouge: 45° / ³⁄₁₆-inch (5 mm)

PATTERN

Page 142

ADVENT WREATH

1 Transfer the pattern and the holes for the candles to the wood plank.

2 Carve out the rounded, cross-shaped inner design with the U-gouge and the bent medium gouge. Always work from the outside toward the center (see page 41). As you work, continually check the depth and correct as necessary. The base should not be thinner than approximately ⁹⁄₁₆ to ¾ inch (1.4 to 1.9 cm).

3 Make the holes for the candles approximately ¾ inch (1.9 cm) deep with the medium gouge and the U-gouge. As you carve, keep checking the precise fit and stability of the candles.

4 Use the stippling tool as described on page 57 to decorate sections of the surface. First tidy up the eight marked surfaces along the lines according to the pattern and mark the stippling surfaces so they are identifiable.

5 Use a template to transfer the stars on the edge and carefully cut them in with a V-gouge: likewise use the V-gouge on the points of the stars and lead them to the deepest point in the center at an angle of approximately 20°. Make this recess as deep as you wish.

TEA LIGHT HOLDER

1 Transfer the design to the block of wood as shown in the illustration on page 43 and saw it out or carve it with the large U-gouge. It's easier to use the mallet in this operation.

2 Draw the outline of the subject on the front side and carve out the front view with the U-gouges.

3 Work the perpendicular base into an oval surface by carving the edges into even curvatures with the U-gouges.

4 Round the couple's upper bodies and heads harmoniously. The groove-like structures can be smoothed with the shallow and medium gouges.

5 Carve the profile of the two heads, the hands, and the head scarf with the V-gouge and smooth them with the shallow gouge (see pages 44–45).

6 Use the medium gouge to make the recess for the tea light. Taper this recess so it is narrower at the bottom and holds the tea light securely.

7 Treat the surface of the subject as you wish or leave it plain.

CANDLE DECORATIONS

Tips and Tricks

◆ It's best to work on the flames if the piece of wood is long enough for two and thus easier to clamp down.

◆ Very thin branches can also be used for the wick and the base pin.

◆ The candles also look pleasing in miniature format with no base pin. Or, extra-large candles are exceptional eye-catchers in flowerbeds or window boxes.

◆ In working with dry floral foam you should use artificial greenery or long-lasting evergreen branches. If you are working with moist floral foam, you can decorate with any kind of winter greenery. The wet floral foam is very absorbent and provides long-term moisture.

DEGREE OF DIFFICULTY

↻

SIZE
Approximately 2 inches (5.1 cm) in diameter, 2¾ to 6 inches (7 to 15.2 cm) tall

MATERIALS
FOR TWO CANDLES
◆ Swiss stone pine or Eastern white pine branch, approximately 2 inches (5.1 cm) in diameter, 8 inches (20.3 cm) long (flames)
◆ 2 birch or hazelwood branches (candles)
◆ Shish kebab skewers (wicks)
◆ Round dowels or shish kebab skewers (base pins)

ALSO NEEDED
◆ Galvanized bucket
◆ Fresh or artificial greenery
◆ Ribbon
◆ Decorative materials, such as nuts, crab apples, and pine cones
◆ Wet or dry floral foam (for securing the greenery and the candles)

CARVING TOOLS
◆ Chip-carving knife
◆ Shallow gouge: 5 sweep ½-inch (13 mm)

1 Cut the branch to the desired length and remove a little bark around the edges. Drill the holes in the center for the stand and the wick. The size of the drill bit should match the diameter of the shish kebab skewer or wooden dowel.

2 Use the shallow sweep chisel to taper the ends of the pine stick until it resembles a flame.

3 Now use a pencil to mark both sides of the stick to a length of 2½ to 2¾ inches (6.4 x 7 cm). Cut in around the marking to a depth of just under 1 inch (2.5 cm) and round the underside.

4 Saw out both flames and carve the rest of the contours with the chip carving knife. The flames should produce an agitated, lively impression. The smooth cuts produce varied, fascinating shadow effects on the flames, depending on how the light hits them.

5 Drill the hole for the wick in the flame. Assemble the flame, wick, candle, and base pin. Make more candles (in different lengths) in the same way. Place a little wet or dry floral foam into the galvanized pail and add the greens and the candles. Decorate with the additional materials and tie the ribbon in a bow around the bucket as shown.

NATIVITY FIGURES

Tips and Tricks

◆ These plain figures look very decorative on a windowsill. The charm of this nativity scene lies in the simplicity of the design and the expressive posture of Mary and Joseph. If you already have some experience you can add simple faces and carve the robes in greater detail.

DEGREE OF DIFFICULTY
◔◔

SIZE
Mary, approximately 5½ inches (14 cm) tall

Joseph, approximately 5¾ inches (14.6 cm) tall

Baby Jesus, approximately 1⅝ inches (4 cm) long

MATERIALS
◆ Boxwood blocks:
Mary, 5½ x 2¾ x 2½ inches (14 x 7 x 6.4 cm)
Joseph, 5¾ x 3½ x 2½ inches (14.6 x 8.9 x 6.4 cm)
Baby Jesus, 1⅝ x ¾ x ¾ inches (4 x 1.9 x 1.9 cm)
Cradle, 2⅜ x 2⅜ x 2⅜ inches (6 x 6 x 6 cm)

CARVING TOOLS
◆ Chisel: 2 sweep ⅜-inch (10 mm)
◆ Shallow chisel: 3 sweep ⅝-inch (16 mm)
◆ Medium gouge: 7 sweep ⅜-inch (10 mm)
◆ Chip carving knife
◆ V-shaped gouges: 45° / ³⁄₁₆-inch (5mm) and ⅜-inch (10 mm)

PATTERN
Page 140

1 Transfer the three individual figures to the wood according to the pattern and saw them out.

2 For Mary and Joseph, draw the centerline on the front side so that the figures' hands and head are centered as seen from the front (see page 43).

3 Joseph: Clamp the figure in the vise. First carve the shoulders, then use the V-shaped gouge to carve and round the arms. Then round the whole figure and carve it cleanly. Important: make sure both arms have the right sweep. Tidy up the face, beard, and hair with the V-gouge.

4 Mary: Clamp the figure in the vice and start by rounding the back. Then carve and round the arms on the front with the V-gouge and the chisel. Set in, carve, and round the face with the shallow gouge. Carve the body. Neaten up the veil and the upper part of the robe with the V-gouge (see pages 44–45).

5 Baby Jesus: Because this diminutive figure is difficult to clamp, it's best to carve it entirely with the chip carving knife. Round the head, cut in along the previously drawn lines for the arms, and carve the garments fairly flat so the arms lie on them. Shape the hands or fists and carve the legs and feet. Proceed very carefully: because of the grain, the feet can easily break off. Finally, clean up the figure.

6 Cradle: Clamp down the cube of wood and draw on the outline of the baby Jesus, following the grain on the topside. Use a medium gouge to carve the hollow in which the figure will lie. Slightly hollow out the long sides of the cube with the shallow gouge. Use the shallow gouge to soften the sharp edges at the head and foot (see photo). You may have to turn the cube around and clamp it again to facilitate the carving. As pictured, make another hollow at the bottom, and then tidy up the whole cradle.

MADONNA AND CROSS

Tips and Tricks

◆ Practice carving faces on pieces of scrap wood or modeling them with clay.

◆ The smaller Madonna is very expressive because of the simple tilt of the head, even though she lacks a detailed face.

DEGREE OF DIFFICULTY (LARGE MADONNA)

◔◔◔

SIZE

Large Madonna, approximately 12 inches (30.5 cm)

Cross approximately 12 inches (30.5 cm)

Small Madonna approximately 7 inches (17.8 cm)

MATERIALS (LARGE MADONNA)

◆ Block of boxwood, 12 x 4 x 3 inches (30.5 x 10.2 x 7.6 cm)

CARVING TOOLS

◆ Shallow gouge: 3 sweep ⁵⁄₈-inch (16 mm)

◆ Medium gouge: 7 sweep ³⁄₈-inch (10 mm)

◆ U-gouge: 10 sweep ³⁄₈-inch (10 mm)

◆ V-gouge: 45° / ³⁄₁₆-inch (5 mm) and ³⁄₈-inch (10 mm)

FOR THE FACE

◆ Chisel: 2 sweep ³⁄₈-inch (10 mm)

◆ Shallow chisels: 3 sweep ³⁄₈-inch (10 mm) and 5 sweep ⁵⁄₁₆-inch (8 mm)

◆ U-gouge: 11 sweep ⁵⁄₆₄-inch (2 mm)

MATERIALS (CROSS)

◆ Planed boxwood board, 8 x 12 inches (20.3 cm x 30.5 cm), 1 to 1¹⁄₂ inches (2.5 to 3.8 cm) thick

CARVING TOOLS

◆ Shallow gouge: 3 sweep ⁵⁄₈-inch (16 mm)

◆ U-gouge: 11 sweep ⁵⁄₆₄-inch (2 mm)

◆ V-gouge: 45° / ³⁄₁₆-inch (5 mm) and ³⁄₈-inch (10 mm)

PATTERNS

Pages 139 and 142

Madonna

1 Draw the outlines of the Madonna onto the wood; if possible have a carpenter saw out a rough blank. The best tool for sawing this out is a band saw; the wood is too thick for a coping saw.

2 Clamp down the rough blank for the figure. Since it's fairly easy to hold the figure from the rear, start the shaping on the front. Based on the lines drawn, lay out baby Jesus and the Madonna's arms and head. In order to get the inclination of the head just right, first draw the centerline of the face and the line for the eyes perpendicular to it. Draw these lines even if no face will be carved. Lay out the shape of the face symmetrically around these lines. The forehead is the foremost point of the figure, along with the hand. Do the rough layout with the 10 sweep ³⁄₈-inch (10 mm) U-gouge; use the 11 sweep ⁵⁄₆₄-inch (2 mm) U-gouge for fine details. Smooth the face with the 7 sweep ³⁄₈-inch (10 mm) medium gouge. Make very fine cuts; for example, on the mouth use the 11 sweep ⁵⁄₆₄-inch (2 mm) and 2 sweep ³⁄₈-inch (10 mm) gouges. Cut in the fingers with the 2 sweep ³⁄₈-inch (10 mm) chisel.

3 Once the front of the figure is laid out, round the back, taking into account the tilt of the head. Then clean up the entire figure (see pages 43–44).

4 Finally, carve the face details of the Madonna and the Baby Jesus. The small Madonna is carved in the same way, but without face and fingers.

Cross

1 Transfer the shape of the cross to the board and saw it out.

2 Draw the body and the panel on the cross; clamp the piece down and use a V-gouge to cut in the contours cleanly. Cut the letters into the panel with the fine U-gouge.

3 Use the shallow gouge to round off the edges of the body and carve the head round.

4 Leave the outer edges sharp, without rounding, to create a greater impression of depth.

5 Finally, sand the sawn edges clean or tidy them up with the shallow gouge.

SIMPLE ANGEL

Tips and Tricks

◆ To keep the base round and even, you can draw a circle with approximately a 2-inch (5.1 cm) diameter on the bottom before you start carving. You will have to keep unclamping the figure to check the base and correct it if necessary. Drawn centerlines, as with the figure in the Workshop on page 43, are likewise helpful in shaping the robe.

DEGREE OF DIFFICULTY
◔◔

HEIGHT
Approximately 6½ inches (16.5 cm)

MATERIAL
◆ Black of boxwood, approximately 7 x 4 x 2½ inches (17.8 cm x 10.2 cm x 6.4 cm)

CARVING TOOLS
◆ Shallow gouge: 3 sweep ⅝-inch (16 mm)
◆ Medium gouge: 16 sweep ⅝-inch (16 mm)
◆ U-gouges: 10 sweep ⅜-inch (10 mm) and 11 sweep ⁵⁄₆₄-inch (2 mm)
◆ V-gouge: 45° / ³⁄₁₆-inch (5 mm)

PATTERN
Page 124

1 With the help of templates, transfer the pattern to the wood as described for the figure on page 43 and saw it out.

2 Clamp the figure down. First lay out the angel from the front by carving out the rough shape. Use the large 10 sweep ⅜-inch (10 mm) U-gouge to carve out the wings; pay attention to the angle of the wings; the side edges of the wings are far back in the wood. The head is far to the front, as are the hands and the front edge of the robe.

3 Next lay out the back of the angel. Establish the thickness of the head and carve away the wood between the wings with the gouge. Likewise remove the excess wood on the head and shape the head with the shallow gouge.

4 Carve the lower part of the robe flat in the rear, using the shallow gouge, so that the figure stands on a base about 2 inches (5.1 cm) in diameter. This gives the wings a more three-dimensional appearance.

5 Draw the sleeves of the robe on the sides and go over the lines with the V-gouge. Use the shallow gouge to carve under the sleeves so that they stand out in relief, then round the sleeves and tidy them up.

6 Finally, neaten up the figure with the shallow gouge; the wings should be approximately ³⁄₁₆ inch (5 mm) thick. Go over the lines of the sleeves and the robe as precisely as possible with the V-gouge so that the resulting curve produces an elegant angel .

POPULAR CARVING DESIGNS FOR KIDS

FIRE-BREATHING DRAGON

1 Transfer the design to the wood, saw it out, and clamp it down.

2 Lower the background evenly between the frame around the design and the dragon to a depth of approximately $9/16$ inch (1.4 cm). First set in the contours of the frame and the figure vertically with the U-gouges to that depth. For tighter spots use the 11 sweep $5/64$-inch (2 mm) U-gouge.

3 Sharpen the contours with shallow and medium gouges. Bevel the frame toward the inside for a distance of a little over 1 inch (2.5 cm).

4 Round the surface of the dragon. First work the head with gentle contours and then deepen the opening of the mouth and tongue with a small U-gouge. Slightly round the eye with the V-gouge, and then carve the claws in relief.

5 Structure the surface. Carve the tongue with the small U-gouge and scale-like depressions on the jaw with the larger U-gouge. Also carve scales in relief on the neck, first setting in the curves of the scales with the V-gouge then structuring and smoothing the surfaces with the shallow gouge.

Stipple the background as described on page 57. Irregularities in hard-to-carve areas will disappear, the background will be harmonious, and the dragon will stand out better.

6 Paint the eye and, if desired, darken the background with diluted light brown watercolor. A white dot for reflected light will make the dragon look lifelike.

DEGREE OF DIFFICULTY
○○

SIZE
Approximately 9 inches (22.9 cm) in diameter, $1^1/8$ inches (3 cm) thick

MATERIALS
- Boxwood board approximately 9 inches (22.9 cm) in diameter and $1^1/8$ inches (3 cm) thick
- Stippling punch
- Watercolors in black and brown
- White primer

CARVING TOOLS
- Shallow gouges: 3 sweep $3/16$-inch (5 mm) and 5 sweep $5/16$-inch (8 mm)
- Medium gouge: 7 sweep $3/8$-inch (10 mm)
- U-gouges: 10 sweep $1/4$-inch (6 mm) and 11 sweep $5/64$-inch (2 mm)
- V-gouge: 45° / $3/16$-inch (5 mm)

PATTERN
Page 125

Tips and Tricks

◆ Screw a board about 16 inches (40.6 cm) long to the back of the disk. You can use C-clamps to secure the projecting ends to the workbench or table for ease of carving.

◆ For hanging, a small hole with the $1/4$-inch (6 mm) U-gouge is adequate. Angle the hole toward the top so that the carving will slide securely onto a nail driven into the wall.

◆ A final varnish will strengthen the impression of gleaming scales on the dragon's neck.

SWEET LITTLE BIRDS

Tips and Tricks

◆ Take advantage of irregular growths known as swirls found in the wood in such places as branching sites.

◆ If you prefer not to carve in your hand, start from a piece of wood large enough to be clamped. Then you can shape the carving with both hands, a shallow gouge, and U-gouges.

◆ These cute, magical birds look fine when left unpainted; you can also paint or varnish them. Since the creatures fit perfectly in the hand, even the smallest children enjoy painting them in bright colors.

DEGREE OF DIFFICULTY
◉◉

SIZE
Approximately 2 to 2½ inches (5.1 to 6.4 cm)

MATERIAL FOR EACH BIRD
◆ Block of boxwood, Eastern white pine, or Swiss stone pine, at least 3 ½ x 2¾ x 2 inches (8.9 x 7 x 5.1 cm)

CARVING TOOLS
◆ Chip carving knife
◆ U-gouges: 10 sweep ¼-inch (6 mm) and 11 sweep ⁵⁄₆₄-inch (2 mm)
◆ V-gouge: 45° / ³⁄₁₆-inch (5 mm)

PATTERN
Page 128

1   These birds are small enough that you can make them from wood scraps of various types. A soft wood with straight grain is a good choice if they will be carved in the hand.

2   Draw the outlines either from the pattern or freehand, and saw out the shape.

3   Shape the point of the beak. Make a fat, round belly and a small, short, slightly upturned tail to produce a squat, pudgy bird. Always carve from the highest to the lowest point (see page 21).

4   Use the 11 sweep ⁵⁄₆₄-inch (2 mm) U-gouge to define the wings and suggest the feathers, then sand to remove any sharp edges. Carve the beak with the chip carving knife, and use the V-gouge if necessary. First saw the open beaks and then shape them with the chip carving knife.

5   Shape the eyes with the 10 sweep ¼-inch (6 mm) U-gouge; they can also be carved in with the chip carving knife.

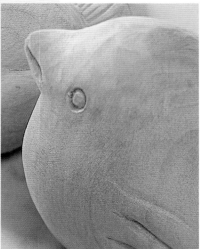

DAGGER & SWORDS

Tips and Tricks

◆ It's best to use a blank about 8 inches (20.3 cm) longer than the finished dagger or sword. That makes it easy to clamp the blank and work on the piece with both hands.

◆ Children can use a rasp and sandpaper to easily turn a rough blank into a little work of art.

DEGREE OF DIFFICULTY

LENGTH
Approximately 12 to 16 inches (30.5 x 40.6 cm)

MATERIALS FOR EACH DAGGER/SWORD
◆ Length of boxwood or eastern white pine, approximately 2 to 3½ inches (5.1 x 8.9 cm) wide and a little less than 1 inch (2.5 cm) thick
◆ Vegetable oil

CARVING TOOLS
◆ Shallow gouges: 3 sweep ⅜-inch (10 mm) and 3 sweep ⅝-inch (16 mm)
◆ U-gouges: 9 sweep 5/16-inch (8 mm) and 11 sweep 5/64 (2 mm)

PATTERN
Page 130

1 Transfer the patterns for the swords or the dagger to the wood and saw out along the outlines.

2 Shape and sharpen the blade with the shallow gouge, and if necessary refine the shape of the blade with a rasp.

3 Carefully smooth the blade with 80- and 120-grit sandpaper.

4 Round the hilt to the desired shape using the shallow gouge and the U-gouges; if necessary, check the symmetry of the two halves of the blade.

5 Use the rasp to slightly roughen the hilt.

6 Apply a final coat of oil or varnish (see pages 55–56) to keep the surfaces from absorbing dirt.

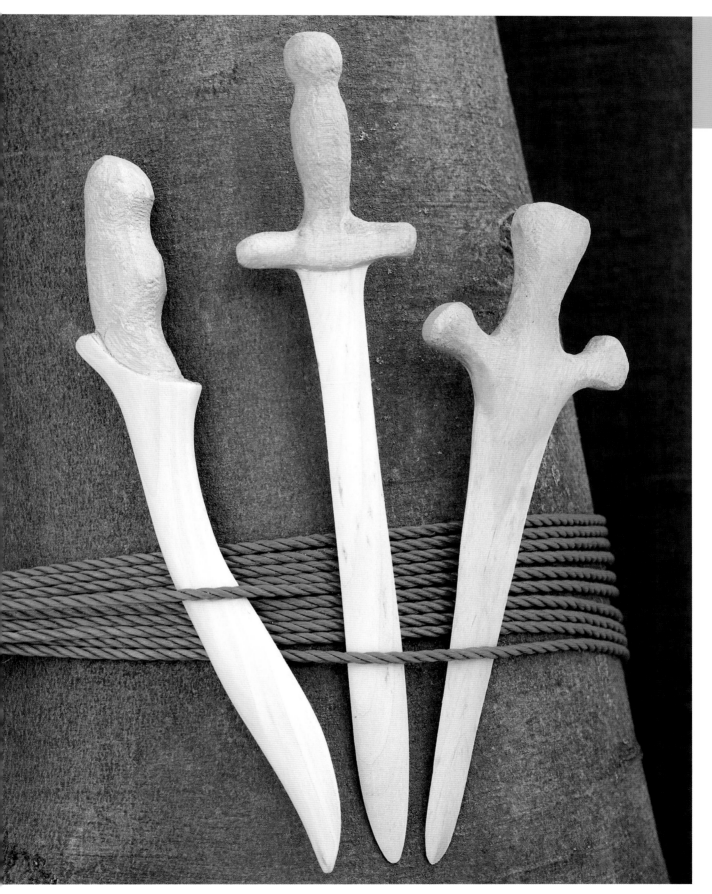

POSEABLE BEAR

Tips and Tricks

◆ The face and the fur structure can be "drawn" permanently with a wood-burning tool. These are available in hobby shops and hardware stores.

◆ The steps in making the bear's body parts are laid out below in clockwise fashion, starting at the lower left.

DEGREE OF DIFFICULTY

SIZE
Approximately 3 inches (7.6 cm) tall, sitting

MATERIALS
◆ Boxwood board approximately 2 x 6 inches (5.1 x 15.2 cm), 2 inches (5.1 cm) thick
◆ Brown felt-tipped pen
◆ 2 rubber bands, each 8 inches (20.3 cm) long
◆ Drill bit, 5/64-inch (2 mm)
◆ Shish-kebab skewers or toothpicks (for gluing the rubber bands)

CARVING TOOLS
◆ Chip carving knife

PATTERN
Page 132

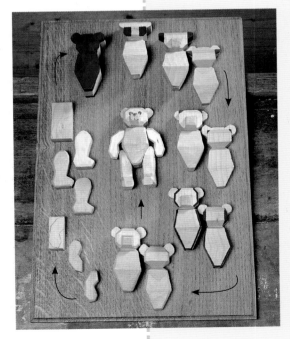

1 Using the templates, draw the arms and legs twice onto the wood and saw them out. Draw and cut out the body with attached head.

2 Use the chip carving knife to slightly bevel the front and rear edges of the arms and legs with smooth cuts.

3 Bevel the legs on the crosshatched surfaces and fit them to the bear's "hips."

4 Draw the side profile of the body and carve it out.

5 Bevel the front and rear edges of the body.

6 Drill through the body, the arms, and the legs at the designated places to accommodate the rubber bands.

7 Insert both rubber bands, folded in half, through the holes. First thread a band through one leg from the outside, through the hip, and then toward the outside through the second leg. Leave a bit of rubber band sticking out on both sides. Use the second rubber band in the same way to attach both arms to the upper body.

8 Use a small peg as long as the hole is deep to glue each end of the rubber band on the arms and legs down flush.

9 So that the arms and legs keep their position under tension, pull the bands on opposite sides and glue them into place with small wooden pegs. Make sure the bands remain under tension and are glued and wedged firmly enough from the outside so they don't slip.

10 Cut off projecting pieces of rubber band or clean up the wood with sandpaper or a rasp.

11 Draw the eyes, nose, and mouth with the felt-tipped pen.

PATTERNS

Note

❧ The patterns are shown slightly reduced in size. It is easy to enlarge them to the size specified in the Project Ideas section, using the provided copy machine percentage or the grid pattern. Also see the instructions on page 22.

Proportions Gauge

The hair stands up over the head.

One head height

Chest

Waist (beltline), elbows

Midpoint of body, wrists

Midpoint of thighs

Knees

Midpoint of calves

Soles of feet

Spatula

Page 31
Pattern on 5/16-inch (8 mm) grid, or enlarge 160%

Box

Page 30
Pattern on 5/16-inch (8 mm) grid or enlarge 160%

Breakfast Board

Page 30
Pattern on 3/8-inch (1 cm) grid or enlarge 200%

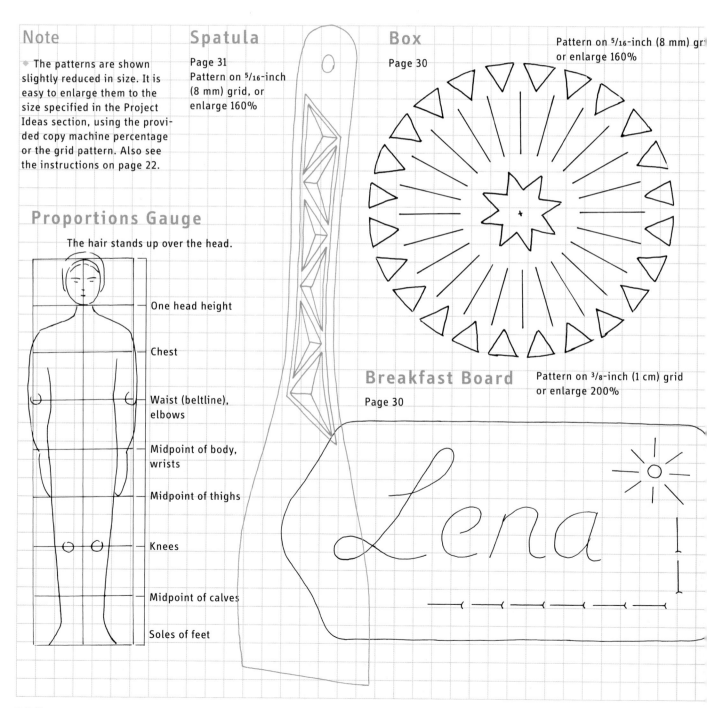

Lena

"Sun Wheel" Bookends

age 31

Pattern actual size

"Celtic Knot" Bookends

ages 38 and 59
attern actual size

Decoration

Page 38

Pattern on ½-inch (1.3 cm) grid or enlarge 250%

A Saying in Relief Carving

Page 39

Pattern on ½-inch (1.3 cm) grid or enlarge 250%

BLEIB STEHEN RENNE NICHT LERNE STEHEN UND WACHSEN WIE EIN BAUM

Daisy in High and Low Relief

Page 39

Pattern on ½-inch (1.3 cm) grid or enlarge 250%

Lettering

Page 33
Enlarge pattern for the alphabet ¼-inch
(6 mm) grid or to 125%

Angel

Front view

Page 113
Pattern actual size

Side view

Fire-Breathing
Dragon

age 114
nlarge pattern
n ¼-inch
5 mm) grid
r to 125%

Bird

Page 46
Pattern actual size

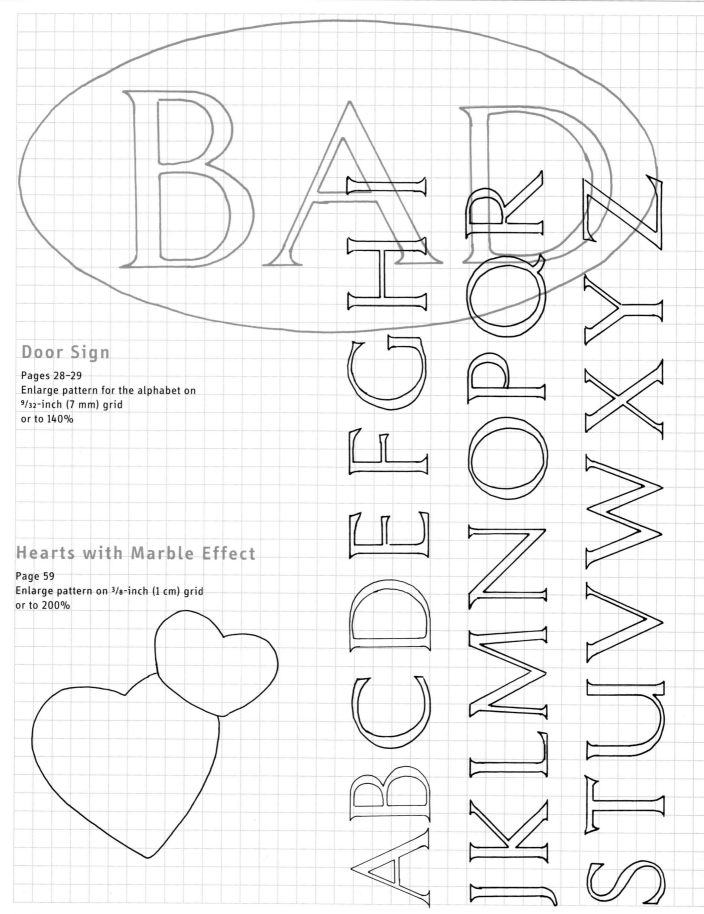

Door Sign

Pages 28–29
Enlarge pattern for the alphabet on
9/32-inch (7 mm) grid
or to 140%

Hearts with Marble Effect

Page 59
Enlarge pattern on 3/8-inch (1 cm) grid
or to 200%

imple Figure
ge 46

Pattern on ³/₈-inch (1 cm) grid,
or enlarge to 200%

Bowl
Page 41

Pattern on ³/₈-inch (1 cm) grid,
or enlarge to 200%

Curvature

Outer
diameter

Goose

Page 52
Pattern actual size

Fond Hearts

Page 53
Pattern on ¼-inch (6 mm) grid,
or enlarge to 125%

Hearts in Two
Colors

Page 58
Pattern on ¼-inch(6 mm) grid
or enlarge to 125%

Letter Opener

Page 53

Pattern on ⁵/₁₆-inch (8 mm)
grid or enlarge to 160%

Classical Figure

age 79
attern on ³/₈-inch (1 cm) grid or
nlarge to 200%

Floral Plate

Page 62

Pattern on 5/16-inch (8 mm) grid or enlarge to 160%

Sweet Little Birds

Page 117
Pattern actual size

Paisley Wall Plaques

Pages 64–65

Pattern on ½-inch (1.3 cm)
grid or enlarge to 250%

Flowers in Relief

Page 67

Pattern on ½-inch (1.3 cm)
grid, or enlarge to 250%

Classical Figure

Page 79

Pattern on ³/₈-inch (1 cm) grid
or enlarge to 200%

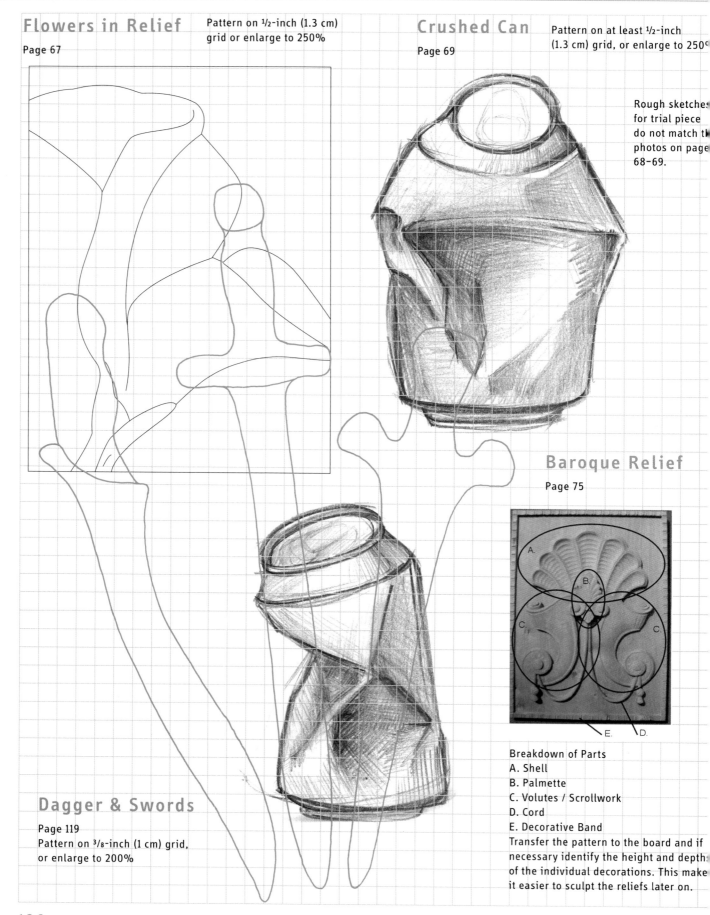

Flowers in Relief

Pattern on ½-inch (1.3 cm) grid or enlarge to 250%

Page 67

Crushed Can

Pattern on at least ½-inch (1.3 cm) grid, or enlarge to 250%

Page 69

Rough sketches for trial piece do not match the photos on pages 68–69.

Baroque Relief

Page 75

Dagger & Swords

Page 119
Pattern on ⅜-inch (1 cm) grid, or enlarge to 200%

Breakdown of Parts
A. Shell
B. Palmette
C. Volutes / Scrollwork
D. Cord
E. Decorative Band
Transfer the pattern to the board and if necessary identify the height and depth of the individual decorations. This makes it easier to sculpt the reliefs later on.

Page 75
Pattern on ½-inch
(1.3 cm) grid, or
enlarge to 250%

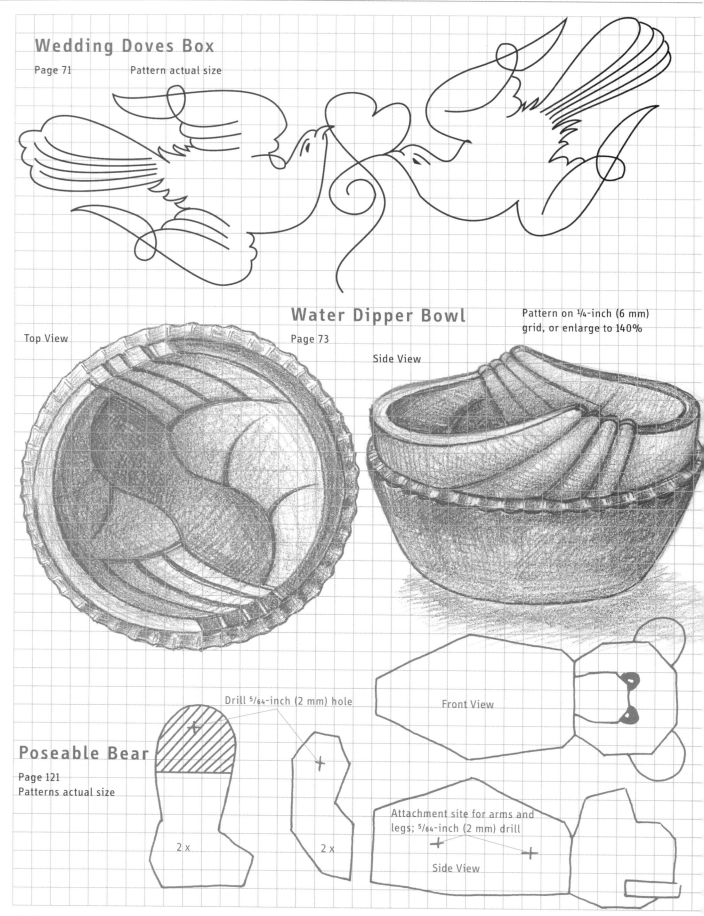

Wedding Doves Box

Page 71   Pattern actual size

Water Dipper Bowl

Page 73

Pattern on ¼-inch (6 mm) grid, or enlarge to 140%

Top View

Side View

Front View

Drill ⁵⁄₆₄-inch (2 mm) hole

Attachment site for arms and legs; ⁵⁄₆₄-inch (2 mm) drill

Poseable Bear

Page 121
Patterns actual size

Side View

2 x

2 x

Organic Candleholders

Page 77

Pattern on ¼-inch (6 mm) grid,
or enlarge to 140%

Side View

Example of Large Candleholder

Top View

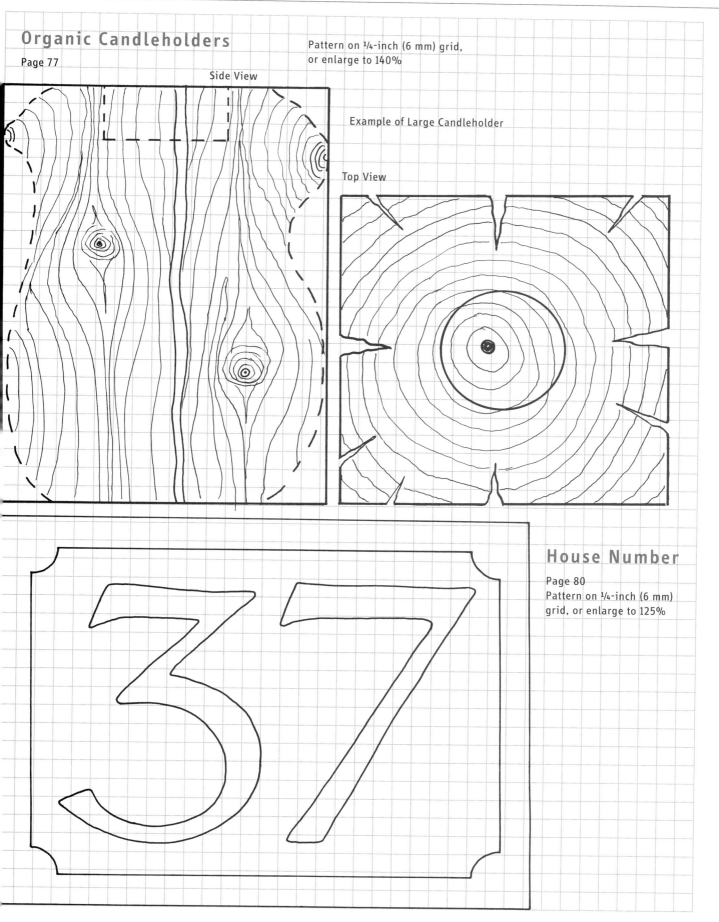

House Number

Page 80
Pattern on ¼-inch (6 mm)
grid, or enlarge to 125%

Door Sign

Page 80

Pattern on ⁵/₁₆-inch (8mm) grid, or enlarge to 160%

Wise Old Owl

Page 83
Pattern on ⁵/₁₆-inch (8 mm) grid, or enlarge to 160%

Snail

Page 85

Pattern on ¼-inch (6 mm) grid, or enlarge to 125%

Green Man

Page 87

Pattern on ⅛-inch (8 mm) grid, or enlarge to 160%

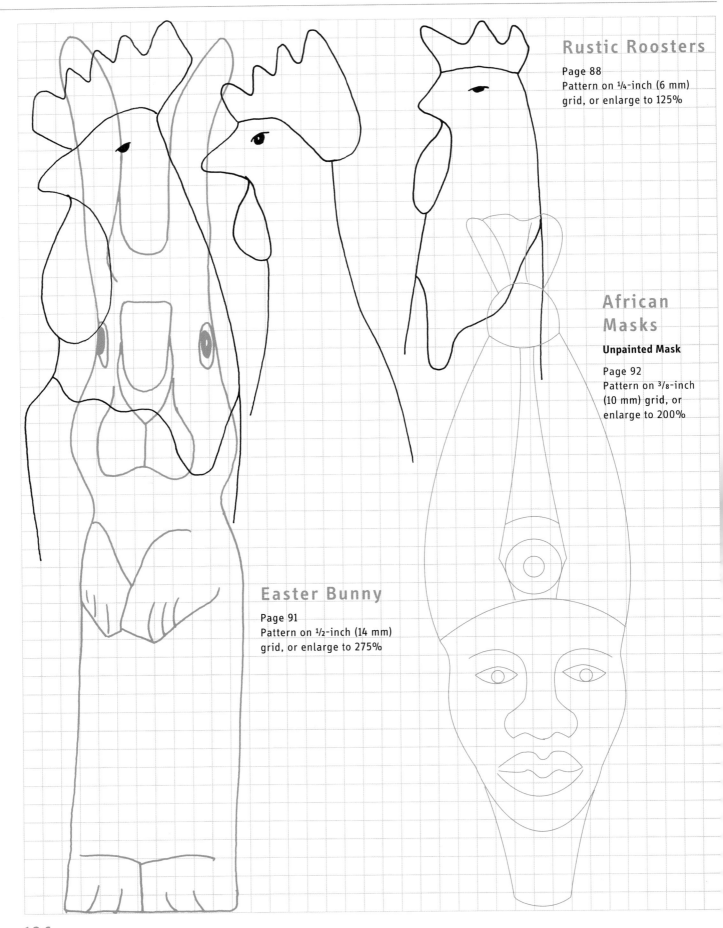

Rustic Roosters

Page 88
Pattern on ¼-inch (6 mm)
grid, or enlarge to 125%

African Masks

Unpainted Mask

Page 92
Pattern on ⅜-inch
(10 mm) grid, or
enlarge to 200%

Easter Bunny

Page 91
Pattern on ½-inch (14 mm)
grid, or enlarge to 275%

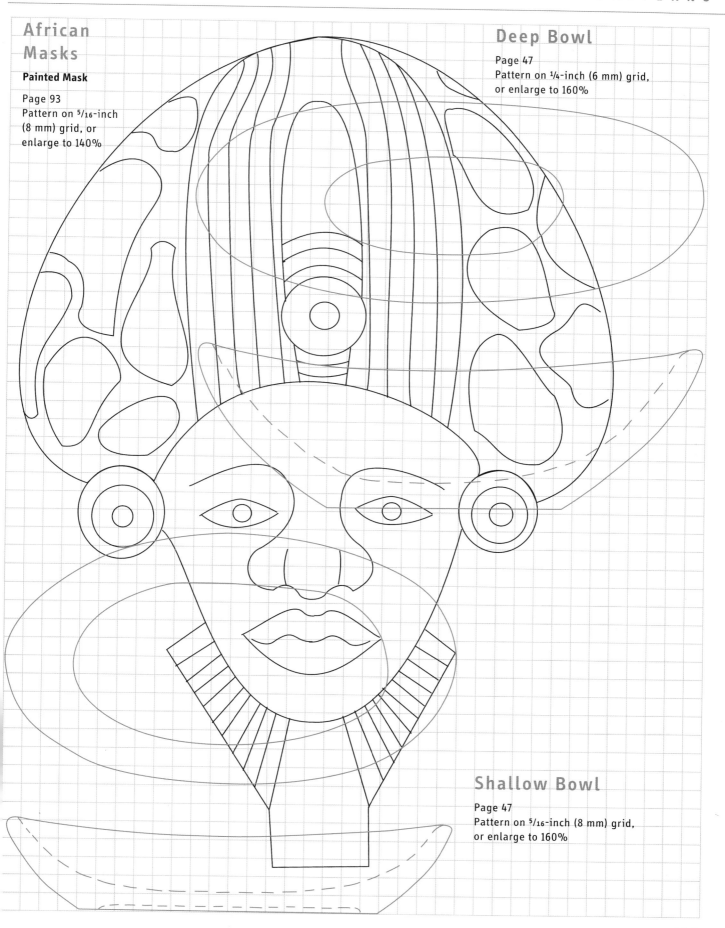

African
Masks

Painted Mask

Page 93
Pattern on 5/16-inch
(8 mm) grid, or
enlarge to 140%

Deep Bowl

Page 47
Pattern on ¼-inch (6 mm) grid,
or enlarge to 160%

Shallow Bowl

Page 47
Pattern on 5/16-inch (8 mm) grid,
or enlarge to 160%

Sun

Page 95
Pattern on ¼-inch (6 mm)
grid, or enlarge to 140%

Colorful Fish

Page 99
Pattern actual size

2 x

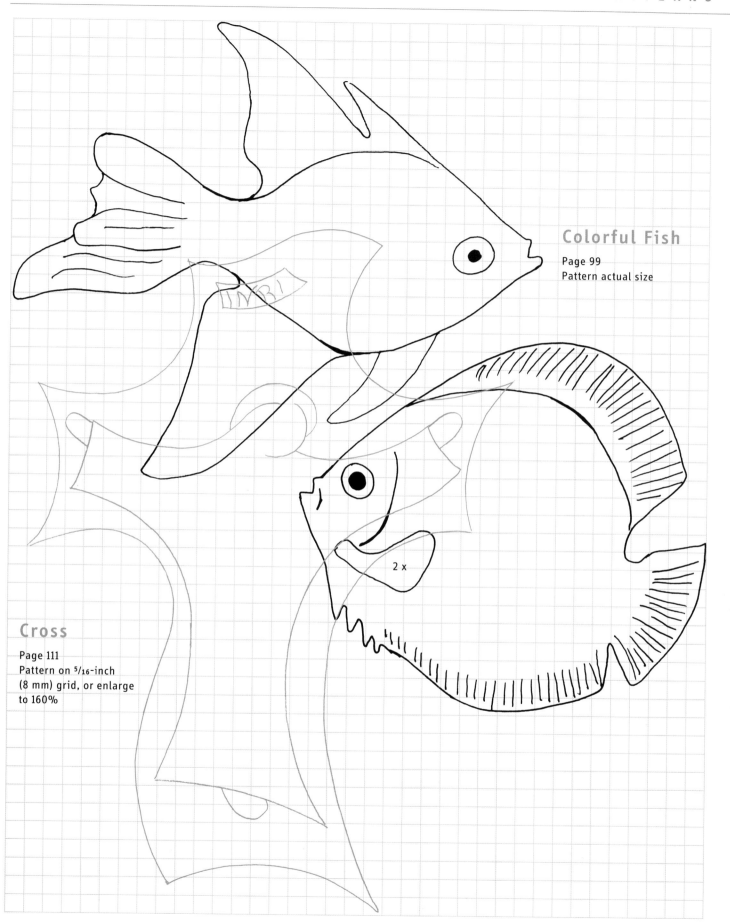

Colorful Fish

Page 99
Pattern actual size

Cross

Page 111
Pattern on ⁵/₁₆-inch
(8 mm) grid, or enlarge
to 160%

2 x

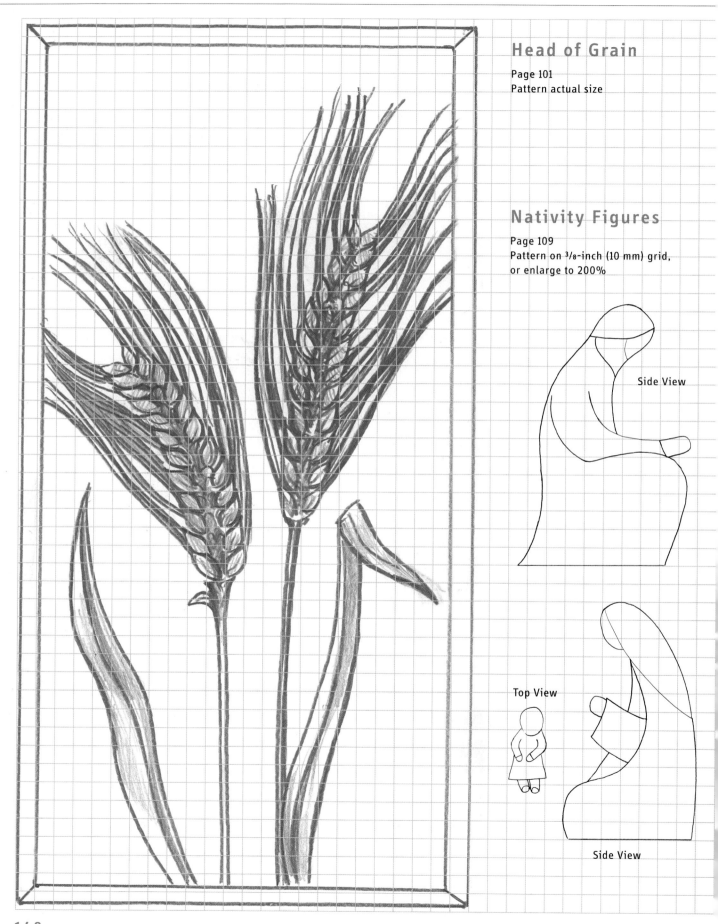

Head of Grain

Page 101
Pattern actual size

Nativity Figures

Page 109
Pattern on ³/₈-inch (10 mm) grid,
or enlarge to 200%

Side View

Top View

Side View

Trees

Page 103
Pattern on ¼-inch (6 mm) grid, or enlarge to 140%

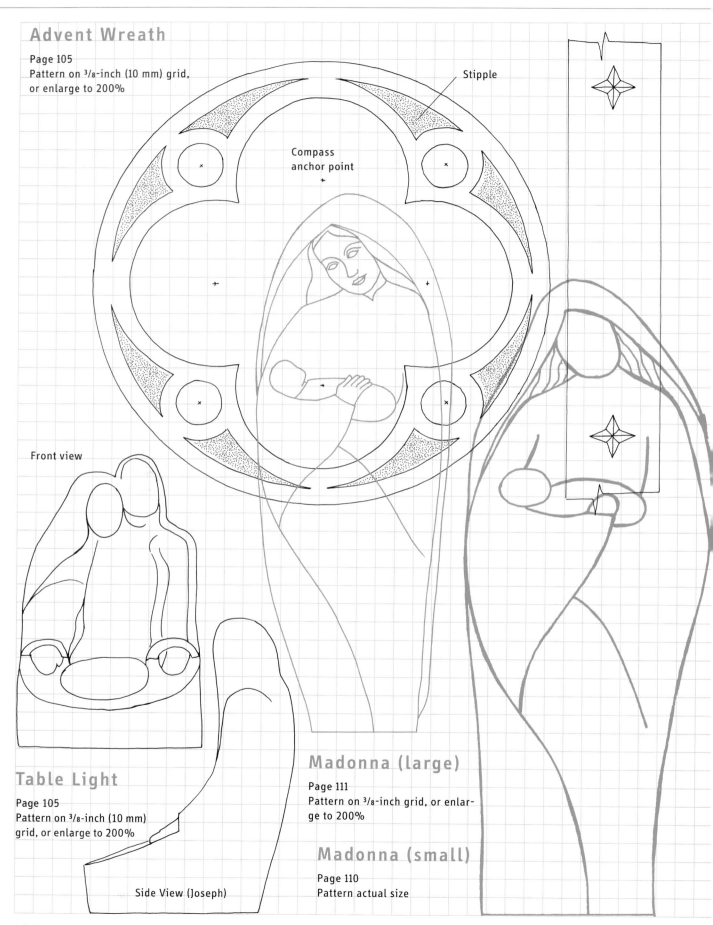

Advent Wreath

Page 105
Pattern on ³/₈-inch (10 mm) grid, or enlarge to 200%

Stipple

Compass anchor point

Front view

Table Light

Page 105
Pattern on ³/₈-inch (10 mm) grid, or enlarge to 200%

Side View (Joseph)

Madonna (large)

Page 111
Pattern on ³/₈-inch grid, or enlarge to 200%

Madonna (small)

Page 110
Pattern actual size

BASIC CHISEL & GOUGE SHAPES
Shapes of Cut and Blade, Sweep Designations

	Cut Shape	Straight Blade	Curved Blade	Bent Blade
Chisel	————	Sweep 1	–	Sweep 21
Skew Chisel	————	Sweep 2	–	Sweep 22 Sweep 23
Shallow Gouge	⌣	Sweep 3	–	–
	⌣	Sweep 4	Sweep 12	Sweep 24
	⌣	Sweep 5	Sweep 14	Sweep 26
Medium Gouge	⌣	Sweep 6	–	–
	⌣	Sweep 7	Sweep 16	Sweep 28
	⌣	Sweep 8	–	–
U-Gouge	⌣	Sweep 9	Sweep 18	Sweep 30
	⌣	Sweep 10	–	–
	⌣	Sweep 11	Sweep 20	Sweep 32
45° V-Tool	V	V-tools come in several angles, such as 45°, 60°, 75°, 100°—in each case, straight, curved, or bent.		

The sweep shapes correspond to the depiction of the cut in the wood. The width of the cutting edge (measured from corner to corner) varies from approximately $1/64$ to $2 1/2$ inches (0.5 to 63 mm), but generally from $5/64$ to $1 1/2$ inches (2 mm to 38 mm).

Sweeps 1 through 11 refer to straight blades. The sweeps with higher numbers come with curved or bent (only forward) blades. Note: not all straight shapes are also available in curved or bent shapes.

Example: Cut 7 is available as a straight gouge (sweep 7), a bent gouge (sweep 16), for projects such as carving bowls, or as a bent gouge. They can be used for carving such things as difficult-to-reach undercuts in decorative high relief.

*Manufacturers of carving chisels have not developed a unified set of designations. Because of hand production, chisels and gouges may deviate from the sweeps depicted. This chart is intended as a guideline to the confusing variety of chisels and gouges and is not definitive.

INDEX

Here are the most important terms, arranged in alphabetical order. The page number provided refers to the main entry in the book.